Yesterday's

I

A Pictorial History
1857 to 1957

LIVERPOOL

Design & Origination: Ian Boumphrey

Published by: Ian Boumphrey The Nook 7 Acrefield Road Prenton
Wirral CH42 8LD
Tel/Fax: 0151 608 7611   e-mail: ian@yesterdayswirral.co.uk
Website: www.yesterdayswirral.co.uk

Printed by: Bookprint SL, Barcelona

ISBN: 1-899241-25-6

**Price
£9.95**

INTRODUCTION

To celebrate our 50th publication I have decided to publish my first topographical book on Liverpool - including City and Suburbs - which covers the years from the 650th to 750th Anniversary of Liverpool receiving its Charter in 1207 ie

1857 to 1957.

Due to the success of my Yesterday's Wirral books, each covering an area of the Wirral Peninsula, I am following the theme of my more recent and most popular books the "Pictorial History" series. These include photographs from my extensive archives and data taken from the annals section at the back of *Kelly's Directories,* which give a brief history of local events and happenings in chronological order. I have sourced other information from local publications, newspapers, booklets, guides etc. and have acknowledged the source where possible. Many of the events mentioned in different publications have conflicting dates and/or information and I apologise in advance for any errors in the 1,000 plus detailed facts listed. In many cases I have used the original terminology and punctuation.

I have illustrated the book mainly with postcards and photographs from my collection and have acknowledged the source on many of them - I have inserted them in the approximate date, as many of them are undated. However, I have acquired many photographs which have no details of origin and apologise for using them without acknowledgement. I hope you approve of my selection of photographs.

BIBLIOGRAPHY

These abbreviations are used in the text as a source reference guide

AISofLRS	An Illustrated Survey of Liverpool Railway Stations	R Gell	1985
APOP	A Pride of Parks	Howard Channon	
BOCOG	Borough of Crosby Official Guide	Crosby Borough Council	1949
BOM	Bombers Over Merseyside	*Liverpool Daily Post & Echo*	1943
CoB	Children of Benares	David Roberts	2003
CofHC	The Opening of the Church of Holy Cross	Church of Holy Cross, Liverpool	1954
CofLOG	City of Liverpool Official Guide	City of Liverpool Corporation	1948
FBPOOB	Formby By-Pass Official Opening Brochure	Lancashire County Council H&BC	1938
HWRLGE	Huyton-With Roby UDC Local Government Exhibition	Huyton-With-Roby UDC	1948
L45	*Liverpolitan* - An Illustrated Monthly Review	Liverpolitan Ltd	1945
LandIM	Liverpool and Industrial Merseyside	Liverpool Chamber of Commerce	1948
LA50A	Liverpool Airport 50th Anniversary	Airport Committee Merseyside CC	1983
LatMVolI	Liverpool and the Mersey Volume1	Ken Longbottom	1995
LCPS	*Liverpool Courier* Property Sales 1874-1907	*Liverpool Courier*	1907
LCS	Liverpool Coronation Souvenir		1953
LDPCE	*Liverpool Daily Post* Centenary Edition	*Liverpool Daily Post*	1955
LOH	Liverpool Official Handbook	Liverpool Corporation	1950
LPS	Liverpool Police Strike	Eleanor Thomas	1986
LTVol2	Liverpool Transport Volume 2 1900-30	JB Horne & TB Maund	1982
MAW	Merseyside at War	Rodney Whitworth	1988
MM&MIB	More Murder & Mayhem in Birkenhead	David Malcolm & Ian Boumphrey	1997
MOL	Memorials of Liverpool	JA Picton	1873
OO	Owen Owen - They Always Come Back	Ian Hargreaves	1968
PAW	Port at War	Mersey Docks & Harbour Board	1946
POIOM	Places of Interest on Merseyside	Merseyside Civic Society	1951
RMSL	RMS *Lusitania*	Booklet	1915
RR&FofL	Road & Rail Ferries of Liverpool 1900-50	J Joyce	1983
TFBL	The Festival Book - Liverpool		1951
TG	*The Graphic* Saturday October 3 1894		1894
THotRaAPoTL	The History of the Royal and Ancient Park of Toxteth Liverpool	Robert Griffiths	1923 edn
TIL	The Ismay Line	Wilton J Oldham	1961
TNTPWOS	The Night The Police Went on Strike	GW Reynolds & A Judge	1968
TSofI	The Story of Irwins 1874-1950	John Irwin	1950
TSOTMTQ	The Story of The Mersey Tunnel Queensway	Mersey Tunnel (Joint) Committee	1934
WHATBG	Where Have All The Breweries Gone?	Norman Barber	1980s
WS	White Star	Roy Anderson	1964

Jan 3   Water from the Rivington Works first introduced into Liverpool for general use

Jan 19   Mutiny on board the American ship *James L Bogart* in the river. One man died from injuries

Feb   Memorial to the late Major Campbell, of two stained glass windows in St Nicholas' Church

Mar 3   A Fancy Dress Ball held in St George's Hall, for the benefit of the charities - proceeds were divided:- Infirmary £250; North Dispensary £150; South Dispensary £160; Northern and Southern Hospital £150 each

Apr 15   Foundation stone for the Free Public Library and Museum laid by William Brown, Esq MP who generously erected it at his own expense - followed by a banquet held in St George's Hall for 500 gentlemen with Tea Parties held in the evening at Concert and Hope Halls

May 10   Cranmer Wesleyan Schools opened Boundary Street

June 12   Wesley Chapel, **Waterloo**, opened

June 21   New Jerusalem Church opened Bedford Street North

July 21   HMS *Hastings* with 60 guns, intended use a guard ship, took up her position in the Mersey

July 26   Cranmer Wesleyan Chapel opened - Vauxhall Road

July 27   The United States Steam Frigate *Niagara* sailed from the Mersey with half the Atlantic telegraph cable which was manufactured in Birkenhead

Sept 1   The new Landing Stage, off the Prince's Pier, opened to the public. Estimated cost £130,000 - 1002ft. long 81ft. wide

Sept 12   Captain Rogers executed at **Kirkdale** gaol for the murder of one of his seamen

Oct 12   Dr Livingstone, the celebrated African traveller, addressed a meeting of merchants in Exchange Buildings

Dec 1   Foundation stone of Holy Trinity Church, Parliament Street, laid - opened 8 August 1858

Dec 16   Two Russian guns which had been captured at Sebastopol, presented by Government and placed in front of St George's Hall - later removed to **Wavertree** Park

Dec 30   St James' Catholic Church opened - **Bootle**

Dec 31   Last meeting of the Dock Committee before their duties passed over to the newly formed Mersey Docks and Harbour Board which met for the first time 5 January 1858

Above: The original Old Everton Toffee Shop

Below: This was an advert from a Liverpool Directory for 'Everton Toffee' which was published just over 100 years after Molly Bushell was established in business in 1753. She invented the toffee, which was world famous, being patronised by Queen Victoria and the Royal Family. By this time the business was run by her grandson, RH Wignall. The advert claims that Mr Wignall was the only person in the world in possession of the original family recipe

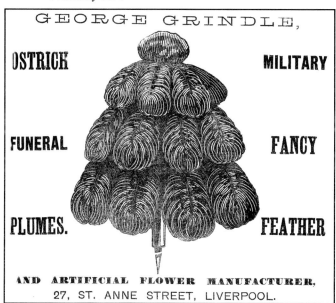

1858/59

Jan 5 — The Mersey Docks and Harbour Board met for the first time - Mr Charles Turner was elected Chairman

Feb 17 — Dense fog caused several collisions in the river. A police constable met his death by falling into Sandon Graving Dock

Mar 10 — The screw-steamer *Pearl* sailed for Africa with Dr Livingstone and party - for the exploration of the Zambezi River

May 17 — The Centenary of the Lyceum Library and News Room celebrated by a soiree held there

May 31 — The Gymnasium and Playground, corner of Chatsworth Street, opened - paid for by CP Melly

Jun 2 — Foundation stone of new Wesleyan Chapel, Grove Street, laid by John Farnworth

July — Polished granite monument erected in Prince's Park in memory of its founder, RV Yates

Aug 9 — Canada Dock opened at the north end of Huskisson Dock

Aug 24 — St Mary's School opened **Edge Hill**

Sept 3 — News received of the successful laying of the Atlantic Telegraph Cable - Queen Victoria transmitted the first message to the President of the United States

Oct — Fire/Police Station transferred to Hatton Garden from Temple Court

Oct 21 — Foundation stone laid for the **Toxteth** Park Workhouse

Dec 30 — Holy Trinity Church **Toxteth** Park consecrated

• — During 1858 - 81,266 persons emigrated from Liverpool

1859

Jan 19 — Fire at Blue Coat Hospital which celebrated its 150th anniversary

Mar 14 — Foundation stone laid of the Infant Orphan Asylum, Melville Place, Myrtle Street by Harmwood Banner

Apr 28 — Packet-ship *Pomona*, left Liverpool for New York and was wrecked that day - only 19 out of 437 were saved.

May 5 — Total cost of St. George's Hall to present time £320,659

Jun — Telegraph wires placed along the line of Docks

Jun 13 — Foundation stone laid for the new Roman Catholic Church in Great Crosshall Street

Sep 16 — Canada Dock opened for traffic by the Cunard steamer *Asia*, Captain Lott at the helm

Oct 26 — *Royal Charter* 2,756 tons auxiliary screw-steamer travelling from Australia to Liverpool with 500 passengers and crew, plus a £400,000 cargo of gold was wrecked off Anglesey - only 35 people saved

Wavertree, a suburban Sub-Post Office is photographed in 1860 - there were two collections a day here at 11.45am and 6.55pm and one on Sunday at 6.45pm - money orders were granted and paid here. The cost of an inland letter under 0.5oz was one penny, under 1oz: two pence and under 2oz: 4 pence

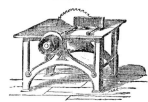

Feb 24 New Reformed Presbyterian Church opened in Shaw Street

Mar 1 Population of Liverpool and Suburbs:- males - 224,082; females - 238,667 = total 462,749. Total number of houses = 75,189

Mar 21 Foundation stone laid for the Jubilee Primitive Methodist Chapel, Yates Street, **Toxteth** Park - to cost £1,350 and seat 400 persons

Mar 21 2,139 paupers in the Liverpool Workhouse

Mar 31 Over 2,269 tons coffee and 23,435 tons sugar in the Liverpool bonded warehouses

Apr 11 New Reformed Church opened Shaw Street

Apr 29 Sailors Home, Canning Place destroyed by fire

May 8 Foundation stone laid for Holy Trinity Church National Schools, **Toxteth** Park - cost £3,350

May 8 Foundation stone laid of the Presbyterian Church, Derby Road, **Bootle** - seating 940 - cost £4,000

June Police Force in Liverpool numbered 982 - annual cost £63,127

June 1 Great Charlotte Street discontinued as a public Market - wholesale dealers only permitted to sell in Queen Square

Jul 2 Street Railway opened from Fairfield to the **Old Swan**

Aug 8 The New Police Courts and Offices, Dale Street, now completely occupied

Aug 29 Funeral of Mr Jesse Hartley, the eminent engineer of the Liverpool Docks

Oct 17 Opening of the new Library and Museum in William Brown Street - A day's holiday was granted and the Liverpool streets were decorated with flags

Nov 1 Church Street widened

Nov 4 Primitive Methodist Chapel opened in Croston Street

*Above: Derby Road, **Huyton** looking south (see 1948)*

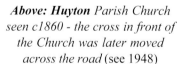

*Above: **Huyton** Parish Church seen c1860 - the cross in front of the Church was later moved across the road (see 1948)*

*Left: **Huyton** Station pictured c1860 on the Liverpool to Manchester Railway - being the first inter-city line in the world when it opened in 1830 (see also 1930)*

1861/62

- Public offices of the **Waterloo-with-Seaforth** Council offices built - later to become the **Waterloo** Town Hall

Census: Liverpool: males - 132,842; females - 136,900. **Everton**: males - 26,078; females - 28,770. **Kirkdale**: males - 7,898; females - 8,237. **West Derby**: males - 24,394; females - 28,364. **Toxteth Park**: males - 32,870; females - 36,414

Apr 5   Meeting at the Town Hall to adopt measures for alleviating the suffering caused by the famine in the north west provinces of India - £2,000 subscribed in the room

June 4   *Great Eastern's* first visit to the Mersey - from New York (*see photo*)

July 2   Street railway from **Fairfield** to the **Old Swan** opened

Aug 17   HRH Prince Alfred arrived in the Mersey from New York via the steamship *Arabia* and proceeded direct to London

Oct 17   The Derby (free) Museum, William Brown Street opened

Nov 1   Church Street widened by taking the south footpath into the carriage-way and opening a corresponding passage for pedestrians through St Peter's Churchyard

1862

Jan 1   **Kirkdale** New Industrial Ragged Schools opened

July 12   Royal Lancashire Militia Barracks opened Rupert Lane cost £13,000

July 12   Lying-in-Hospital Myrtle Street opened

July 29   The celebrated Confederate war steamer *Alabama*, built in **Birkenhead** left the Mersey for America

Oct   Brocklebank Dock & North Carriers' Dock opened

Dec 8   New Timber Dock, north end of Canada Dock, opened

Above: The steam-ship *Great Eastern's* first entry into the Mersey, June 4 1861. She made the passage from New York, with a large cargo and 212 passengers, in 9 days 11 hours. She had six masts, five funnels, and both screw and paddles—her crew numbered 397. She sailed on her first voyage from Liverpool, with troops and cargo for Canada, June 27. Returned to the Mersey, August 15, having left Quebec on the 6th. Sailed again from this port for New York. September 10th, under command of Captain Walker, having on board 175 cabin and 193 steerage passengers. On the following Thursday, during a heavy gale, when about 280 miles to the west of Cape Clear, her steering apparatus became deranged and broken, for two days and nights the vessel was exposed to a terrific sea. Great damage was done to the interior fittings. On the following Tuesday she arrived off Queenstown.

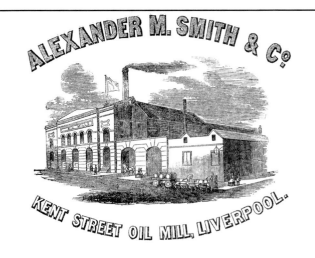

1863

Jan 1 The New Liverpool Savings Bank, Bold Street, opened for business

Jan 6 St James-the-Less Church Gore Street opened

Jan 24 New Lifeboat *Rescue* launched - witnessed by over 50,000 people

Feb 13 St John's Wesleyan Chapel opened

Mar 10 Marriage of the Prince of Wales with the Princess Alexandra of Denmark. This national event was celebrated in Liverpool by every possible demonstration of loyalty by the authorities and the inhabitants (*see article this page*)

Apr 27 Liverpool Cemetery **Anfield** Park was consecrated by the Bishop of the Diocese

May 16 The Wellington Column at the top of William Brown Street inaugurated with a salvo of 19 guns

May 21 St. Catherine's Church opened Tunnel Road, **Edge Hill**

1864

Jan 15 A terrific explosion of gunpowder took place on board the ship *Lotty Sleigh* bound for Africa - having taken in about 11 tons of gunpowder from the magazine boats lying off **Tranmere**. No lives were lost, but property was destroyed both sides the river

Feb 15 London & North Western Railway extended from **Speke** to **Edge Hill** with new stations at **Allerton** and **Mossley Hill**

June 1 Cheshire Lines Railway extended from **Garston to Brunswick** with stations at Mersey Road & **Aigburth**, **Otterspool** and **St Michaels**

The marriage of the Prince of Wales with the Princess Alexandra of Denmark took place on 10 March 1863. This national event was celebrated in Liverpool by every possible demonstration of loyalty by the authorities and the inhabitants. The chief features in the proceedings were - the Corporation's entertainment of 60,000 children, at a cost of £1,500, a volunteer procession, boat races on the river, bands in the **Wavertree** Park, free music at St George's Hall and at night, splendid illuminations in the town, fireworks in the outskirts, and the brilliant lighting up of HMS *Majestic* in the river. In the afternoon the Mayor, RC Gardner, Esq, gave a splendid banquet at the Town Hall, to the elite of the town and neighbourhood, and at night, a Grand Ball, which was both numerous and brilliant, the Exchange Newsroom and the Underwriters' rooms being connected with the Town Hall by covered galleries for the occasion

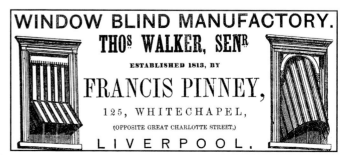

1865/66

Apr 21   Harmwood Banner died - he was a great benefactor to charitable institutions including orphan asylums

May 15   Remains of trenches made by Prince Rupert's army at the siege of Liverpool 1644 discovered in London Road

Oct 7   New hospital opened 17, Islington Flags for the treatment of cancer and skin diseases

Oct 31   Prince and Princess of Wales visited the town, the Free Library and Museum

Nov 6   New gymnasium in Myrtle Street opened by Lord Stanley

1866

Jan 12   Great snow storm broke the poles and telegraph lines for about 60 miles between Liverpool and London

Jan 13   Foundation stone laid for the *New Theatre and Opera House* Lime Street by Miss Titiens

May   Epidemic outbreak of cholera in Liverpool

May 4   Screw ship *Helvetia* bound for New York with emigrants on board, returned to Liverpool due to an outbreak of cholera on board

June 1   First section of **Bootle** branch opened for goods by London & North Western Railway between **Edge Hill** and **Tuebrook**

June 21   Duke of Edinburgh started three day visit - he attended the regatta on the Mersey; the training ships; St George's Hall and laid foundation stone for the Children's Infirmary, Myrtle Street

July 6   Islington Vegetable Market removed to the Haymarket

Aug 27   Lancashire & Yorkshire Railway opened North Mersey branch between North Docks and **Aintree** and **Fazakerley**

Sept 19   The *Great Eastern* arrived in Liverpool after successfully laying the Atlantic cable

Oct 1   Grand Banquet held to celebrate the success of the Atlantic cable layers and a telegram was sent to the President of the United States

Oct 15   *Prince of Wales Theatre* (later *Royal Alexandra*) opened in Lime Street

Oct 15   LNW **Bootle** branch completed between **Tuebrook** and Canada Dock for goods traffic

Oct 18   Christ Church **Bootle** consecrated - cost £8,000

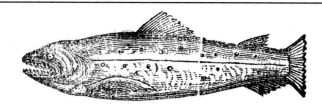
Work started on creating **Sefton** Park on 26 March 1867 when the Corporation purchased about 375 acres of land off the Earl of Sefton for £251,177 – from the foot of the hill, bounded by Ullet Road and Smithdown Road on the north and east. Linnet Lane, Aigburth Road and Aigburth Vale Road on the south and west. In order to get a good approach from Aigburth Road and Lark Lane to the park, an additional piece of land of 12 acres was purchased for £12,000. The Corporation offered premiums of 300 guineas, and 150 guineas for the best plans, open to the world. There were 29 competitors who responded to the invitation. The first premium was awarded to the joint design of Mr Andie, landscape gardener of Paris, and Mr. Lewis Hornblower, architect of Liverpool. The second premium was awarded to Mr Milner of London.

1867

•		Watson Prickard, men's tailors, established in Liverpool
Feb 15		Emmanuel Church, West Derby Road consecrated - cost £15,000
Mar 26		Work started on creating **Sefton** Park (*see article*)
June 12		Stanley Park - design of Mr Kemp of Birkenhead adopted - cost of land was £120,000 and laying out, together with cost of bridges, lodges etc estimated at £40,000
Aug 12		New **Waterloo** and Corn Warehouse Docks opened
Oct 9		Holy Trinity National Schools erected - cost £2,000
Dec 4		Town Council resolved that about 1,000 men be employed on forming **Sefton** Park - wages not to exceed 2/- per day
Dec 13		Charter of Incorporation granted to the Township of **Bootle**[BOH]
Dec 30		**Bootle** made a Borough Corporate

1868

Feb 5		Serious fire at St Nicholas' old Church
Mar 16		**Bootle** appointed first Mayor - Mr Chas Howson
May		The Committee of the Northern Hospital passed a resolution 'That the organ now in the operating room be moved to the Chapel'[LNH]
July 16		St Paul's Church (North End) consecrated – Lord Derby gave the land & £1,000 to the endowment fund

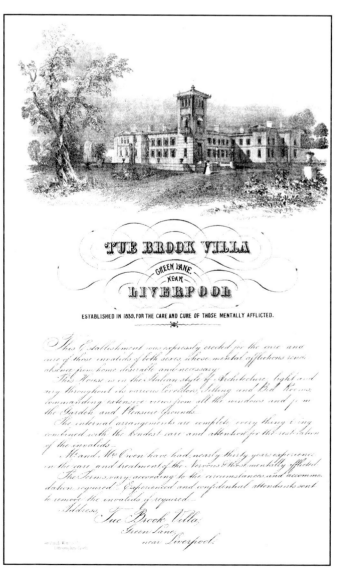

1869/70/1

Apr 1   **Runcorn** railway Bridge opened, shortening the route of the LNW to Crewe and the south by six miles

Apr 10   Grand Banquet given to Charles Dickens in St George's Hall

July 17 St Nathaniel's Church, Pine Grove consecrated

July 20 St Margaret's Church, Princes Road consecrated

Sept 28 Statues of the Earl of Derby and Joseph Mayer, unveiled in St George's Hall

Oct 21   St Saviour's Church, Breckfield Road consecrated

Nov 1   Omnibus Tramway opened from the **Dingle** to the Town Hall

Dec 14   Cabmen's Shelter, Pierhead opened (built by public subscription)

1870

May 14   **Stanley** Park officially opened by the Mayor

July   Bank Hall Station opened on the Lancashire & Yorkshire Railway line[ISOLRS]

July 1   Passenger train service provided between **Edge Hill** and Canada Dock with a new station at Breck Road

July 21 Christ Church, **Kensington** consecrated

July 31 New Church of St Stephen, Byrom Street consecrated

Aug 14   St Nicholas' Church, **Blundellsands** opened for public worship

Sept   **Wavertree** Station opened on the London & North Western Railway line[ISOLRS]

Sept 1   Omnibus Tramway opened to Spellow Lane, **Walton**

Nov   **Edge Lane** Station opened on the London & North Western Railway **Bootle** branch[ISOLRS]

Nov 3   Statue of Queen Victoria unveiled by the Mayor

Dec 16   Wesleyan Methodist Chapel opened Rice Lane, **Walton**

1871

Mar 1   Census taken:- total population of Liverpool and suburbs: males 240,228 and females 253,177 = 493,405

Mar 1   The North Western Railway Hotel Lime Street opened

Mar 2   Maiden voyage to New York of the White Star Line steamer *Oceanic*[WS] (*see photo*)

Apr 27   Christ Church Linnet Lane consecrated

May 20   St John's the Baptist Church **Tuebrook** consecrated

Sept 11 Seamen's Orphanage, Orphan Drive, **Newsham** Park - foundation stone laid

Nov 16   New Church of St Anne, Great Richmond Street, consecrated

Dec 1   George's Dock Basin closed, for the purpose of commencing the new approaches to the river

Dec 30   St Ambrose's Church Prince Edwin Street, consecrated

Above: The White Star Line steamer Oceanic *seen in full sail. She and her sister ships* Atlantic, Baltic *and* Republic *were all launched or had their maiden voyages in 1871; these pioneering ships rendered all other Atlantic steamships obsolete overnight. They were built by Harland and Wolff, Belfast - who went on to build all White Star Line ships. The maiden voyage to New York of the* Oceanic *was on 2 March 1871[WS + TIL]*

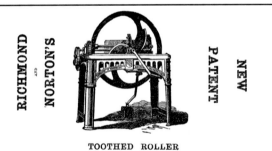
Liverpool College.

MIDDLE SCHOOL.

Report of the Attendance, Conduct, and Progress of ......*C. Brunner*...... Class *IV*

for the Month ending *May 31* 1870

TIMES ABSENT ...*9*...   TIMES LATE ...*0*...

Conduct *Fair - very talkative in class*

Divinity	*Good*
English	*Good*
Latin	*Fair*
French	*P. Fair*
German	*P. Fair*
Mathematics	
Arithmetic	*V. good*
Nat Philosophy	
Drawing	*Fair*
Writing	*V. Fair*
Bookkeeping	
Vocal Music	*Fair*

Monthly Holiday *allowed*

...............Head Master.

Above: This Report of the attendance, conduct and progress was for a boy in the Middle School of Liverpool College (see 1909)

1872

Jan 1	L&NW Railway Co Branch line opened from **Huyton** to **St Helens**
Feb 17	New Sunday School building, St Andrew's Scotch Church, opened in Rodney Street
Feb 27	St Bridget's Church, Bagot Street, opened in **Wavertree**
Mar	Emigration during this month from Liverpool was 14,374 persons carried in 58 ships (almost two per day)
Apr 10	**Bootle** Hospital, Derby Road opened by Lord Derby
May 20	HRH Prince Arthur (Queen Victoria's third son) opened **Stanley Park** - followed in the evening by the Mayor's Banquet at the Town Hall
May 21	HRH Prince Arthur opened the new Royal Southern Hospital and then a flower show at **Sefton** Park, in the evening there was a Fancy Dress Ball at St George's Hall
June 7	The old man-of-war ship, the *Tees*, which had been used as a Mariners' Church, for 45 years, sank in St George's Dock
Aug 15	Public houses first closed at 11pm
Oct 24	Maiden voyage of the White Star Line steamer *Celtic* to New York[ws] (*see photo*)
Nov 5	Institute for Infectious Diseases, Netherfield Road North, **Everton,** opened by the Mayor
Nov 7	Banquet given at the Town Hall to HM Stanley, the intrepid discoverer of Dr Livingstone in Africa

1873

•	West Lancashire Golf Club founded, adjoining Hall Road Station, **Blundellsands**
•	Henry Tate completed the building of his new Sugar Refinery in Liverpool - produced 400 tons refined sugar per week[LDPCE]
Mar 1	**Cressington** Station (from 1877 known as **Cressington & Grassendale**) opened on Cheshire Lines Committee line[ISOLRS]
Mar 5	St Cuthbert's Mission Church, Robson Street, **Everton** opened for Divine service
Apr 3	Large meeting of working men at Newsome's Circus, Whitechapel, in aid of Mr Plimsoll's exertions to stop sending overladen ships to sea [the Plimsoll Line]
May 1	New L&NW Railway Co route opened between Liverpool & Chester via the **Runcorn** Bridge
May 21	Consecration of St James the Less Church, Stanley Road
June 17	Citizens of Liverpool turned out *en masse* to welcome the Shah of Persia who paid a visit to Liverpool
Aug 9	Convalescent Institution opened at **Woolton**
Oct 16	Grand Banquet at the Town Hall given by the Mayor to the Earl of Derby - attended by the *elite* of the town and neighbourhood
Nov 25	St Margaret's Church, **Anfield** consecrated
Dec	Dreadful accident at **Broad Green** Railway station, the Brazilian Vice-Consul killed

Above: This is a view in the Mersey of the White Star Line steamer Celtic, *whose maiden voyage to New York was on 24 October 1872. This was one of the last of the slim-line pioneer steamers of Ismay's White Star Line[ws]*

1874

- John Irwin opened his first shop at 101, Westminster Road **Kirkdale** [see 1950][TSOI]
- Feb 11 Church of St Stephen's, **Gateacre**, consecrated
- Mar 2 Liverpool Central and St James Stations opened on the Cheshire Lines Committee line[ISOLRS]
- Mar 2 Brunswick passenger station closed on the Cheshire Lines Committee line - replaced by Central Station in Ranelagh Street [ISOLRS]
- Apr 1 **Garston** Station opened on the Cheshire Lines Committee line[ISOLRS]
- Apr 16 Steble Street Baths opened
- May **Hunts Cross, Halewood** and **Hough Green** stations opened on Cheshire Lines railway[ISOLRS]
- June 25 White Star Line steamer *Britannic* sailed from Liverpool on her maiden voyage to New York (*see advert for steerage passengers*)
- July 13 St Philemon's Church, **Toxteth** Park, consecrated
- July 23 The old George's landing stage removed and replaced the following day with the new one
- July 27 The new landing stage approaches open to the public
- July 28 The new landing stage destroyed by fire - estimated damage of £250,000 (*see photo on opposite page*)
- Sept 28 HRH Duke of Edinburgh (Queen Victoria's 2nd son) visited Liverpool to lay the foundation stone for the Walker Art Gallery - he also opened the Seamen's Orphanage which was close to where he stayed at *Newsham House*
- Sept 28 Grand Bazaar held in **Stanley** Park for one week to raise funds for the Stanley Hospital which was opened by the Mayor - unfortunately the weather being stormy, the tents were blown down - despite the weather over £1,000 was raised

Above: This is an advert showing the layout for the emigrants' steerage accommodation on the White Star Line steamers the Germanic *and* Britannic *which were both launched in 1874; at £200,000 they were not cheap - but were well built by Harland & Wolff and value for money - the* Britannic *survived until 1950! The steerage passengers were provided with berth* (separated into single women; married couples & families; and single men) *also unlimited supply of well-cooked food but they had to supply bed, bedding, plate, mug, cutlery and water-can* (this was normal for all shipping lines then and it was White Star that later first introduced an all-in price which abolished the sorry scenes of emigrants carrying their bedding and crockery around with them). *The First Class passengers paid more but lived the life of luxury*

Above left: A horse bus is seen in Aigburth Road, Liverpool about 1874 - although the picture is blurred, the rear view shows that the upstairs passengers, some of whom can be seen wearing top hats, are sitting on two seats the length of the bus, back to back, known as 'knife board' seats

Left: Richmond Terrace, **Everton,** photographed in 1877 - a horse and cart is seen in the road to the right of a group of children

Above: Crowds are gathered on the steps of St George's Hall with street traders awaiting custom bottom left

Above: St John's Church can be seen in the centre, to the rear of St George's Hall - the church was closed in 1897 and St John's Gardens built on the site

Above: The burnt-out timbers of the Liverpool landing stage are viewed following the fire which destroyed it, the day after it was opened to the public on 27 July 1877 - the estimated cost was £250,000

Above: The sign beneath the funnel states "Fare One Penny Birkenhead Park Docks and Street Railway Woodside" - the seating on the upper deck of this paddle steamer runs the length of the ship back-to-back with most passengers choosing to sit facing the river

1875/6

- FL Calder College of Domestic Science founded (originally known as the Liverpool Training School of Cookery) - first set up to train ladies to teach the poor how to cook. It was decided that it was more productive to teach the children as their mothers were too set in their ways[THoFLCC]

Mar 4 All Saint's Church, Broad Green Road, **Old Swan**, consecrated

June 23 St Matthew & St James's Church, **Mossley Hill**, consecrated

July 5 His Highness, the Sultan of Zanzibar stayed at the North Western Hotel during his four day visit

Dec 29 Statue of SR Graves, former Liverpool MP, unveiled in St George's Hall

1876

Apr Georges landing stage completed and reopened following fire (*see 1874*)

Apr **Bootle** Village and Millers Bridge L&Y stations replaced by new Bootle (Oriel Road) station

June 21 New church at **Speke** consecrated by the Lord Bishop of Chester

Aug 10 New Church of All Hallows, **Allerton**, consecrated

Nov 13 Hengler's Grand Circus opened in West Derby Road, Liverpool by Mr Charles Hengler - who became renowned for bringing the best in international entertainers to the city (*see also 1895*)

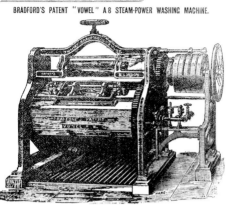

Above: *Castle Street before mechanised vehicles*

*Above: William Rathbone's Statue in **Sefton** Park was Unveiled 1 January 1877*

VETERINARY & SHOEING FORGE,
11, COLLEGE LANE, LIVERPOOL.

HORSES EXAMINED FOR SOUNDNESS.

GEORGE MORGAN,

MEMBER OF THE ROYAL COLLEGE OF VETERINARY SURGEONS, EDINBURGH
AND LONDON.

Above: A Gala Concert held at St George's Hall following the opening of the Walker Art Gallery by the Duke of Edinburgh[TG]

Right: Crowds outside the Walker Art Gallery which was opened by Lord Derby 6 September 1877[TG]

1877

- **Huyton-With-Roby** constituted as a Local Government district - population *c.*4,000
- Work commenced on building TW Thorougood's Brewery in **Waterloo** - completed 1878[WHATBG]

Jan 1   William Rathbone's Memorial Statue unveiled in **Sefton** Park (*see photo*)

Apr 11   Corporation Baths opened in Archer Street and Westminster Road

July 9   *Rotunda Theatre*, Scotland Road, burnt down - damage estimated at £35,000

Sept 6   The Walker Art Gallery presented to the town by the Mayor Mr AB Walker and opened by Lord Derby - the day was a general holiday and a Grand Banquet was held in St George's Hall in the evening (*see picture*)

Oct 10   YMCA in Mount Pleasant inaugurated

Nov 20   St Peter's Church, **Aintree** consecrated

Nov 22   St Cuthbert's Church, Robson Street, **Everton** consecrated

1878

Feb 6   Auction - *Dublin Vaults,* ph. + house & 3 cottages Great Crosshall Street - sold £2,050[LCPS]

May 6   Auction - *The Loggerheads* ph. + shop & 4 cottages 172-174 Richmond Row - sold £3,620[LCPS]

May 9   Auction - *The Royal William* ph. 2 Crown Street sold £2,870[LCPS]

Jun 26   Auction - *Park Hill Hotel* bh. + 3 houses, Parr Street - sold £410[LCPS]

Jun 27   New buildings of Merchant Taylor's School opened

Jun 27   Auction - *The Eddystone* ph 15 Parker Street - sold £9,600 - by 1907 their licence had been extinguished[LCPS]

July 24   'Rock House Estate' including 'Rock House' and 3 houses in Lower Breck Road - sold £18,000[LCPS]

Aug 2   Lodge Lane Public Baths opened by the Mayor

Aug 22   North End Branch of the Sailor's Home opened

Aug 22   Auction - *Royal Standard* ph. shops + houses, Fox Street **Everton** - sold £10,000[LCPS]

Sept 10   Congregational Church, Marmaduke Street, **Edge Hill** opened for Divine Service

Oct 11   Panic at the *Colosseum Theatre*, Paradise Street where 37 people were trampled to death

Oct 29   Liverpool College for Girls opened at **Huyton**

Dec 11   Auction - shop, brewery + 4 houses High Street **Wavertree** - sold £1,410[LCPS]

1879/80

- The *Liverpool Daily Post* launched a new evening paper the *Liverpool Echo*
- **Feb 6**   Reform Club opened in Dale Street
- **May 3**   The Steble Fountain, opposite the Art Gallery, formerly handed over to the Corporation
- **May 3**   The Sanitorium in connection with the Seaman's Orphanage in **Newsham** Park was opened by the Mayor
- **Oct 8**   The Picton Reading Room opened - built by the Corporation at a cost of £20,000 and named after James Allanson Picton JP, FSA in recognition of over 30 years of public service - a Banquet was held in the evening at St George's Hall, in honour of the occasion
- **Nov 13**   Auction - *Bush Vaults* ph. 93 Grafton Street - sold £950[LCPS]
- **Dec 1**   Cheshire Lines North Liverpool line between **Hunts Cross** and **Walton-on-the-hill** opened with stations at **Gateacre**, **Childwall**, **Knotty Ash** and **West Derby**[ISOLRS]
- **Dec 11**   Auction - *The Mariners* - Cable Street built 1856 - sold £1,205[LCPS]
- **Dec 17**   *The Shakespeare* ph. 43 Whitechapel - sold £4,300 - later re-built[LCPS]

1880

- **Blundellsands** Tennis Club founded
- **Jan 1**   Alexandra Dock Station opened on the London & North Western Railway line[ISOLRS]
- **Jan 22**   HRH Princess Louise visited Liverpool to take the SS *Sarmation* to Canada
- **Apr 15**   New Dental Hospital opened in Mount Pleasant
- **May 20**   *Salisbury Arms* ph. Salisbury Street - sold £5,080[LCPS]
- **June 17**   'Penketh Hall' Smithdown Road - sold £4,000[LCPS]
- **July 1**   Cheshire Lines Railway extended from **Walton-on-the-Hill** to Huskisson for goods (and passengers on 2 August)
- **July 13**   Cheshire Lines North Liverpool line extended to **Aintree** Central
- **July 21**   Meeting held in the City Hall to raise funds for a University College for Liverpool - £80,000 promised
- **Aug 19**   Auction - *Royal Amphitheatre* Great Charlotte Street sold £20,000 [re-built as the *Royal Court Theatre*][LCPS]
- **Sept 1**   Pownall Square Market (the oldest in Liverpool) discontinued by order of the City Council
- **Sept 3**   Mr Warrington Wood's statue of Sir Andrew Barclay Walker unveiled in the Walker Art Gallery
- **Nov 30**   St Athanasius' Church, **Kirkdale**, consecrated
- **Dec 21**   Auction - 'Quarry' + 8 houses Quarry Road **Stoneycroft** Reserve £3,000 not met[LCPS]

1881

Jan	River Mersey froze and ships had to battle through thick ice [LDPCE]
Census:-	The population of Liverpool and the suburbs was 611,075 (an increase of 117,670 since 1871)
Feb 25	Auction - *The Clock* ph. Scotland Road - sold £1,675[LCPS]
Mar 1	**Garston** Church Road Station opened on the London & North Western Railway line[ISOLRS]
Apr 23	New Government offices opened in Victoria Street
May 1	Nearly 60,000 emigrants passed through Liverpool in the first four months of this year
June 10	An attempt to blow up the Town Hall by the Fenians was foiled by two policemen who were rewarded
July 14	Auction - *Black Horse* ph. Soho Street + 7 houses Tarbock Street - sold £2,960[LCPS]
July 27	St Cyprian's Church, **Edge Lane** consecrated
Aug 11	New tramways opened to **Old Swan** and **Wavertree**
Aug 24	Auction - *Breck Hotel* Breck Road - sold £2,590[LCPS]
Sept 1	**Bootle** (Balliol Road) LNW station opened to give connections between **Edge Hill** and **Southport**[AISOLRS]
Sept 8	New North Docks opened by HRH the Prince of Wales including the Langton and Alexandra Docks - the day was observed as a general holiday
Sept 10	*Royal Court Theatre* (formerly the *Royal Amphitheatre*) opened in Great Charlotte Street
Oct 6	Auction - *Boundary Hotel* ph. Lodge Lane - sold £3,400[LCPS]
Oct 29	Mayors of Liverpool and **Birkenhead** officiated at the commencement of building the Mersey Railway tunnel
Dec 1	Auction - *Preston Arms* ph. St James Street - sold £1,100[LCPS]
Dec	Auction - *The Old Musty*, shops & warehouse Church Street - sold £22,000[LCPS]

1882

•	The Ramblers Football club was founded in **Crosby**
Mar 2	Auction - **Halewood** Brewery + adjoining house and following public houses:- *Hunts Cross Hotel* **Hunts Cross**; *Lord Raglan* + 2 houses, Window Lane **Garston**; *Barley Vaults* High Street **Wavertree**; *Horse Shoe* **Whiston**; *Churn Inn* Tontine Street **St Helens**; Beerhouse and cottage **Thatto Heath** and Beerhouse and cottage, Quarry Street **Woolton** - sold £17,6000
Apr 10	Town Hall, **Bootle**, opened
Apr 26	Auction - *Mersey Vaults* - ph. 59-61 Kirkdale Road **Kirkdale** - sold £4,000[LCPS]
Apr 26	Auction - *County Court Vaults*,+ offices, stables etc 75-79 Lime Street - sold £14,100[LCPS]
Apr 29	New Hospital for Incurables, Dingle Head opened
June 6	Auction - *Crown & Grapes* ph. Houghton Street - sold £2,400[LCPS]
June 16	*Old House At Home* ph. + 2 cottages Waterloo Street **Wavertree** - sold - £430[LCPS]
July 11	**Bootle's** first tramway opened from Marsh Lane to Lime Street [RR&FoL]
Sept	**Spellow** Station opened on the London & North Western Railway[ISOLRS]
Oct 30	**Gateacre** Village Institute and Club opened
Nov 8	Auction - 'The Harrington Lime Works' Hill Street **Toxteth Park** - sold £2,750[LCPS]
Nov 16	Auction - 'Everton Quarry' Oakfield Road, corner Walton Breck Road **Anfield** - sold £3,200[LCPS]

*Above: The men are sitting on a wall outside **Bootle** (Oriel Road) Station which replaced two stations in 1876 opened to give connections between **Edge Hill** and **Southport***

1887/88

May 16   HRH Princess Louise (Marchioness of Lorne) opened the Church especially built for the deaf and dumb, Prince's Boulevard - then opened the Jubilee Exhibition in Edge Lane which closed in October

May 24   **Gateacre** received the following gifts from Sir AB Walker to celebrate the Queen's Jubilee:- A marble bust of the Queen, The Village Green on which it stands and the **Gateacre** Institute, Library and Reading Room

May 26   Auction - *The Grove Hotel* ph. Rimrose Road - sold £16,100[LCPS]

June 2   The Queen of Hawaii, accompanied by her daughter (Princess Liliuokalani) and suite were entertained by the Mayor

June 3   Auction - *Queen Anne Hotel* + bowling green ph. Fazakerley Road **Walton** - sold £4,000[LCPS]

June 17   Auction - *Park Hill Hotel* ph. + shop & 3 houses 69-75 Parkhill Road - sold £7,450[LCPS]

June 21   The Queen's Jubilee was celebrated with a general holiday, illuminations and decorations and included special services in local churches; a march-out of the local Volunteers; a procession of Trades and Friendly Societies, by dinners to the aged, poor and those in hospitals and workhouses

June 22   **Bootle** Free Library and Museum opened by the Mayor of Bootle

June 30   Auction - *George Hotel* ph. 129 Whitefield Road **Everton** - sold £1,630[LCPS]

June 30   **Bootle** Police Force commenced their duties

June 30   *The Beehive* 52 Upper Beau Street - sold £1,205[LCPS]

July 5   A Jubilee treat was given to 90,000 children who visited the Jubilee Exhibition in Edge Lane over three days

July 9   20,000 school children 'Jubilized' in local parks

July 28   Auction - *Omnibus Inn* ph. St Oswald Street **Old Swan** - sold £2,450[LCPS]

Aug 2   St Benedict's Church, Kepler Street, consecrated

Aug 24   Auction - *Stanley Hotel* ph. + 3 shops & 10 cottages 442 Rice Lane - sold £7,000[LCPS]

Aug 28   **Bootle** Hospital new wing extension opened by Thomas Ismay

Sept   Auction - *The Royal Hotel*, built 1878, 45 Dale Street - sold £42,000 [later London & Lancashire Insurance Offices][LCPS]

Sept 6   Over the next month, the Mayor was to distribute 94,616 Jubilee Medals to elementary school children

Dec 16   Statue of Major-General Earle, erected by public subscription, was unveiled

1888

•   **Everton** Founder Members of the Football League

Jan 2   Mersey Railway extension opened, bringing **Wallasey**, **Hoylake** & **West Kirby** into direct communication with Liverpool

Jan 11   The Prime Minister, The Marquis of Salisbury, as a guest of Mr AB Forwood MP, Financial Secretary, visited the Conservative Club; attended a demonstration at *Hengler's Circus* followed by a Banquet at the Philharmonic Hall

Feb 7   'The Beehive Brewery' + 4 houses 58-62 Upper Beau Street - sold £2,510[LCPS]

Mar 23   HRH Prince of Wales attended the Grand National at **Aintree** as a guest of the Earl of Sefton

May 7   **Bootle** Balliol Road Public Baths opened by the Mayor

June 29   Auction - *London Tavern* ph. + 2 shops 45-47 Ranelagh Street - sold £11,300[LCPS]

June 30   The Liverpool Commercial Banking Company amalgamated with the Bank of Liverpool Ltd

July 7   **Knotty Ash** Bowling Green presented as a gift to the village by Mrs SH Thompson of Thingwall Hall

Aug 10   Channel Fleet visited the port and performed some Naval manoervres

Aug 15   Auction - *The Toxteth* 141 Park Street - sold £5,050[LCPS]

Aug 27   *New Shakespeare Theatre* opened in Fraser Street

Sep 28   Auction - *The Rimrose* ph. Rimrose Road - sold £6,500[LCPS]

Sept 30   Some 202,243 emigrants left Liverpool for America and Canada for the first nine months of 1888

Nov 20   The *Great Eastern* steamship sold at auction piecemeal over five days - sale amounted to £58,000

Nov 22   The City Hospitals for Infectious Diseases opened in Netherfield Road and Grafton Street by the Mayor

Dec 24   *New Theatre Royal* opened in Breck Road, **Everton** - could accommodate 1,100 people

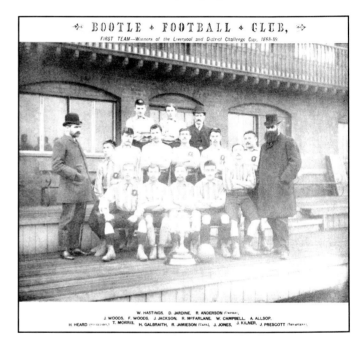

Above: **Bootle** *Football Club - players and officials for the 1889/90 season - winners of Bootle & District Challenge Cup*

Above: The **Woolton** *Gas Works are seen in Rodick Street, Woolton*

1889

- **Bootle** General Hospital presented with a horse ambulance
Feb 8   Auction - *Swan Hotel* 12 & 14 Cazneau Street - sold £13,100[LCPS]
Feb 8   Auction - *Royal Standard* 59 Cazneau Street - sold £7,000[LCPS]
Mar 6   Auction - *Bleak House* ph. + 6 houses 131 Parkhill Road - sold £5,250[LCPS]
Mar 29   HRH Prince of Wales attended **Aintree** Races
Apr 30   Auction - *Newsham Park Hotel* West Derby Road - sold £8,100[LCPS]
May 18   Memorial Church of St Dunstan, Earle Road, **Edge Hill** consecrated
Aug 7   Maiden voyage from Liverpool to New York of the White Star Line Armed Merchant Cruiser *Teutonic* (*see photo*)[WS]
Aug 15   Auction - *Halton Castle* ph. and 'Hayes Cottages' 40-42 Mill Lane - sold £4,250[LCPS]
June 4   New Wholesale Fish Market opened in Great Charlotte Street
July 31   Florence Maybrick tried at the Assizes, St George's Hall, for poisoning her husband, James Maybrick of **Aigburth** and was sentenced to death - later commuted to penal servitude
Sept 3   Auction - *Dewdrop Inn* ph. withdrawn £2,000, Reserve £2,100 - re-built and re-offered as *The Empire* 8 October 1896 Hanover Street - sold £8,250[LCPS]

Above: The 10,000 ton pioneer White Star Line Armed Merchant Cruiser Teutonic *sailed on her maiden voyage from Liverpool to New York on 7 August 1889 - she survived the First World War and was scrapped in 1921*[WS]

1890

Feb 5   New Church of St John the Evangelist, Breck Road (known as the Groves Memorial Church), consecrated
Mar 5   The Liverpool Dock labourer's strike - lasted 26 days - 20,000 men paraded the streets - the military called out
Apr 14   Mail Coach Service re-established by the Post Office between Liverpool and Manchester
May 13   Cottage Homes, **Fazakerley**, erected by the **West Derby** Board of Governors, formally opened
June 23   New Police Court buildings opened by the Mayor
July 3   Auction - *Blundell Arms Hotel* Blundellsands Road West - built 1862 - sold £6,100[LCPS]
Aug 2   New mortuary at the south end of Prince's landing stage erected jointly by the MD&HB and City Council
Aug 14   **Bootle** became a County Borough - boundaries amended and name changed from **Bootle-cum-Linacre** to Bootle[BOH]
Oct 2   The Balfour Institute, Smithdown Road opened
Oct 9   **Knotty Ash** Village Hall and Club opened by Earl Derby
Oct 23   **Woolton** Free Public Library opened
Oct 29   New Royal Infirmary, Pembroke Place opened by HRH the Duke of Clarence - followed by an evening Ball
Dec 2   St Philip's Church, Sheil Road, consecrated

Above: This Pegram's Tea advert in the shape of a tea cup had a calendar for 1890 on the reverse (See 1891 advert)

*Right: In 1889 the owner of the Farmer's Arms was described as:- 'William Wright Beerseller & Weighing Machine Keeper 54, Woolton Street, **Woolton**'. The sign above the door says 'Farmer's Arms - William Wright - Licensed to sell Ale, Porter and Tobacco - To be drunk on the premises'*

1891

- BICC became the first company in the British Empire to manufacture paper insulated cable
- Feb 18   Auction - *Brewer's Arms* bh. Deysbrook Lane - sold £1,550[LCPS]
- May   **Everton** FC Division 1st Division Champions 1890/91
- June 24   A Violent thunderstorm damaged St Paul's, St Jude's and St Margaret's Churches and St Saviour's Schools, Canning Street. Sewers and water pipes burst flooding Paradise Street, Temple Street, Byrom Street etc.
- Census: The population of Liverpool and the suburbs was 617,032 (an increase of 5,957 since 1881)
- Aug 28   Auction - *Cross Keys* ph. 41 Moorfields - sold £1,760[LCPS]
- Sept 8   Auction - Fire Station + house 1-3 The Green, London Road - sold £800[LCPS]
- Sept 15   Auction - *Canning House* ph. 145 London Road - sold £4,850[LCPS]

*Above: Crosby Station was opened on the Liverpool, **Crosby** and Southport Railway in 1848*

Above: This Pegrams Tea advertising calendar for 1891 - in the shape of a tea pot - had a picture of a lady on the reverse (See also 1890 advert)

Above: The Cunard liner Catalonia *is seen berthed at Liverpool. Built in 1881 by J&G Thompson, Glasgow, she operated on both the Liverpool to New York and Boston routes. She also helped to transport troops to the Boer War - she was scrapped in 1901*

- Liverpool FC founded
- Auction - 'Otterspool Estate' **Otterspool** - sold £55,000[LCPS]

Jan 11   Mersey Railway extended from James Street to Liverpool Central Low Level

Feb 1   The Liverpool Naval Exhibition was held at the Walker Art Gallery

May 28   The Olympia Theatre & Circus, Overton Street, **Edge Hill** totally destroyed by fire

June   **Sefton** Park Station opened on the London & North Western Railway[ISOLRS]

June 30   *Black Bull Inn* ph. 2 Warbreck Moor **Walton** - sold £6,750[LCPS]

July 14   HRH the Duke of Connaught visited the city where he resided at Newsham House - he called at the Seaman's Orphanage; then the Southern Hospital; on to the Town Hall where he inaugurated the Vyrnwy Water Supply to Liverpool - he pressed an electric button which set in motion two magnificent temporary fountains which were later illuminated by electric light

July 29   The Liverpool Lifeboat capsized during a fearful storm when going to the relief of the *Maxwell* - two of the crew were drowned and another later died

Aug 3   J Bibby & Son's Oil Mills & Warehouse, Formby Street were destroyed by fire - estimated loss £50,000

Sept 29   **Aintree** racecourse grandstand destroyed by fire

Nov 9   'The Huyton Quarry Iron & Steel Works' **Huyton Quarry** - sold £4,400[LCPS]

Nov 16   Liverpool University Jubilee Clock Tower set in motion by the donor, Mr WP Hartley - cost £1,000

Dec 1   The Nautical College in Colquitt Street opened by Lord Brassey

Dec 3   Honorary Freedom of the City conferred on the Prime Minister, Rt. Hon. WE Gladstone, at St George's Hall - afterwards Luncheon at the Town Hall

Dec 17   Opening of the Victoria Buildings, Victoria College, Victoria University [later part of Liverpool University] by Earl Spencer, Chancellor of the University

*Above: Two preachers are standing on a platform in front of this travelling Gospel Mission Car No.31 'Charity', which was photographed in the 1890s by the **Formby** photographer SB Reynolds*

Above: This horse tram is heading for Pier Head having come from Green Lane via West Derby Road. The building to the left of the tram on the corner of Church Street and Whitechapel later became Bunney's famous store

Above: The horses pull their load along the Dock Road, as workmen are building the new Liverpool Overhead Railway

1893

Jan 7   Terrible fire in Juniper Street where three warehouses were all ablaze at one time - two firemen were killed

Feb 4   Official opening of the Liverpool Overhead Railway, by the Rt Hon the Marquis of Salisbury followed by luncheon at the Town Hall

Mar 23   Auction - *The Victoria Hotel* ph. St Johns Lane - sold £13,250[LCPS]

Apr 23   Earl of Derby died at **Knowsley** aged 67

May 11   Auction - *The Talbot Hotel* + houses - 8 Vernon Street & 20-24 (licence extinguised) - sold £1,460[LCPS]

June 2   Auction - *The Grapes* ph. 8-10 Milton Road - sold £290[LCPS]

June 22   Auction - 'Windsor Brewery' - Upper Parliament Street sold £10,000[LCPS]

Aug 3   Great fire at Canada Dock where four timber yards were destroyed - estimated damage £100,000

Nov 6   The Lord Mayor gave a Banquet to the United States Ambassador

Nov 27   Foundation stone laid for St Margaret's Higher Grade Schools at **Anfield**

Above: *T Bruce Ismay, later to control White Star Line after his father Thomas died in 1899 and survivor of the* Titanic *disaster in 1912, lived here at Sandheys, Mossley Hill Road, with 10 acres of ground, from 1893 to 1920[TIL]*

Above: *Wheeler & Wilson, whose premises were at 73, Bold Street, advertised "The best and cheapest sewing machines in the world" with prices from £5.10 shillings*

Below: *This pony and trap is heading for the Custom House Station on the Liverpool Overhead Railway*

- Marine Football Club founded at **Crosby**
July 25 Auction - *Masonic Arms* 39 Berry Street built 1837 - sold £685[LCPS]
Sept 10 HRH The Duke of York laid the foundation stone for the new Post Office to be erected in Victoria Street
Oct 10 Auction - *Tam O' Shanter* ph. 4 houses, lock-up shop + 4 cottages 167-173 Vauxhall Road - sold £700[LCPS]
Oct 13 First Merseyside Derby Liverpool FC v Everton FC - Everton won 3 - 0 at Goodison in front of a crowd of 44,000
Nov 1 Church of St Gabriel, **Huyton Quarry**, Consecrated
Dec 7 Auction - *Grove Hotel* ph. built 1891 at 112-114 Falkner Street - sold £3,750[LCPS]
Dec 12 Auction - *Original Plough Inn* ph. Scotland Road - sold £1,395[LCPS]
Dec 13 Bishop O'Reilly's Memorial Schools, Leyfield Road, opened - building cost £10,000

Above: This superb photograph was taken over 110 years ago in Eaton Road, **West Derby** - the road which led to Knotty Ash

Above: Two cottages are seen in Alder Road, **West Derby**

Below: These horse-drawn cabs are heading towards the Liverpool Overhead Railway from Pier Head

Above: A policeman is posing by the horse tram at Derby Road bridges - the weather must be good as the upstairs is full - note the reversible seats face the front of the tram

1895

- Derby Park opened in **Bootle** - 22 acres
- May 14 New system of using locomotives to convey goods between South Docks station and North Docks stations replacing horses and wagons
- June 12 Mersey Docks & Harbour Board line opened including Riverside (Pier Head) Station - the first passengers to use this station embarked on the White Star steamer *Germanic* sailing to America (*see below*)
- June 15 The first direct train from London to Riverside Station
- July 3 Auction - 'Brown Moor Farm', Endbutt Lane, **Great Crosby** - sold £925[LCPS]
- July 10 New Riverside Station for Atlantic passengers, formally opened at Prince's Dock
- July 28 Auction - *Omnibus Inn* ph. St Oswald Street, **Old Swan** - sold £2,450[LCPS]
- Aug 1 Auction - *The Grapes* ph. 18 Upper Dawson Street - sold £3,150[LCPS]
- Nov 6 Auction - *Carnarvon Castle* ph. Tarleton Street - sold £4,835[LCPS]

Above: The White Star steamer Germanic *is berthed at Riverside (Pier Head) Station - its passengers were the first to use this station for embarking, before sailing to America - the steamer had just received an overhaul in Belfast*

Above: Joseph Jones & Co (Knotty Ash) Ltd, **Knotty Ash** *Brewery, East Prescot Road, was founded in 1869 and registered in September 1924. The brewery was taken over by Higsons Brewery Ltd in 1937 with over 70 public houses*[WHATBG]

Above: Passengers are waiting at the landing stage for the paddle steamer to dock; a liner is seen in the background

Left: A programme for **Hengler's Grand Cirque**, *West Derby Road, Liverpool for the twice daily performance - which included 12 acts of which the last one being the Pantomime "Aladdin" - was dated 9 January 1895 - the sole proprietor was Mr Albert Hengler who also designed the scenery and produced the whole of the spectacle. Albert Hengler's father, Charles, was a travelling showman from Denmark who opened a circus in Dale Street in 1855 but was forced to close down in 1861 - then opened another in Newington the same year, which was later demolished. He returned to Liverpool and opened Hengler's Grand Cirque in 1876. The running of the circus was taken over by his son Albert and continued through to 1901 when it was sold and the new* Royal Hippodrome Theatre *opened in 1902 (see November 1876)*

- Sandon Dock Station closed - replaced by Huskisson Dock and Nelson Dock Stations on the Liverpool Overhead Railway[ISOLRS]
- Langton Dock Station opened on the Liverpool Overhead Railway[ISOLRS]

Jan 4 Liverpool Cotton Exchange opened - celebrated by a Banquet

Jan 16 Auction - *The Alexandra Theatre* + 3 shops, Lime Street - sold £30,100 [became the *EmpireTheatre*][LCPS]

June 17 Auction - *Steel Grey* ph. + shop & 3 houses 106 Pitt Street - sold £800[LCPS]

Apr 14 Auction - *Cathedral Hotel* houses & shops built 1860 Church Lane - sold £4,750[LCPS]

June Thorougood Brewery **Waterloo**, was registered as TW Thorougood Ltd[WHATBG]

July 1 The Corporation purchased the property, rights, powers and privileges of the Liverpool Electric Supply Co for £400,000

Aug 4 Death of Bertha Lewis, the widow of David Lewis (*see 1885*) and a further £100,000 was reverted to the 'David Lewis Charity Fund'

Sept 1 Drinking Fountain erected in Shaw Street Public Gardens - in memory of Edward Whitley MP

Sept 1 Liverpool Crematorium opened in Priory Road, **Anfield**

Sept 24 Auction - *Boundary Vaults*, built 1840 + 3 shops & 6 cottages Falkner Street - sold £3,100[LCPS]

Oct 5 The Palm House at **Sefton** House formerly opened

Oct 6 Liverpool and Bootle Police Orphanage opened at Sunnyside, **Woolton**

Oct 19 Foundation stone laid for the Northern Hospital

Nov 19 *Sheil Park Hotel* ph. + shop, 207-209 West Derby Road - sold £6,000[LCPS]

Nov 25 First cremation at the new **Anfield** Crematorium

Dec 2 Auction - *Queen's Arms* ph. + shop 91-95 St Oswald Street **Old Swan** - sold £5,320[LCPS]

Dec 20 Liverpool Overhead railway extended to Dingle and Herculaneum station rebuilt further north

Below: This shows both sides of an advertising book mark for the 'Standard Umbrella' - the front side being a young lady in the arm of a very smart soldier in full uniform and the reverse side advertising the latest umbrellas available from their shop at 69, Church Street, Liverpool - with prices

***Above: Aintree** Wesleyan Methodist Mission Hall, Eastbourne Road (the sign for the road can be seen on the side of the wooden building), corner of Warbreck Moor*

***Above:** Taken in 1890s, the nearest horse tram was built in the 1880s and was bound for New South Docks - it was cheaper to travel outside on some trams - the seats upstairs on this tram being the 'knife-board' type which are back-to-back running the length of the tram*

***Above:** Wavertree Mill was a 'post mill'. The wooden structure stood on a brick base and could be rotated on a central pivot, by turning a wooden lever, so the sails could face the prevailing wind. The first mention of a mill here was in 1452 and was the property of the crown for about 200 years. It was last worked about 1890, finally being demolished in 1916*

1897

- Morton Garden opened in Stanley Road **Bootle** as a Rest Garden with over one acre of land[BOH]

Mar 5 — Auction - *Audley Arms* Aubrey Street **Everton** & 6 Houses - sold £570[LCPS]

Mar 17 — The Liverpool Corporation agreed to purchase the Liverpool Tramway Company for £567,375

Apr 1 — The jetty at the north end of the Prince's landing stage was opened

Apr 13 — *The Grapes* Public House and stable, corner Marybone & Alexander Pope Street - sold at auction for £550[LCPS]

May 20 — *Horn of Plenty* bh. 248-250 Whitefield Road **Everton** - sold £6,750[LCPS]

May 31 — *Cressington Hotel* in Aigburth Road **Grassendale** sold at auction for £4,750[0LCPS]

May 31 — Auction - *Phoenix Hotel* Brunswick Road + house & 6 Shops - sold £9,500[LCPS]

June 22 — Queen Victoria's Diamond Jubilee Day (*see this page*)

June 16 — Auction - *Old Pilot Boat* ph. 23-25 Denison Street - sold £1,900[LCPS]

July 29 — Auction - *Old Ivy House* ph. + 3 houses 60-66 Marybone - sold £1,770[LCPS]

Sept 1 — Liverpool United Tramways and Omnibus Co acquired by Liverpool Corporation[LTVol2]

Dec 26 — Last services held at St George's Church - the site was acquired by the Corporation for re-development

Below: The Cunard liner Campania *is pictured at the Liverpool landing stage in 1897. She was launched 8 September 1892 with her maiden voyage from Liverpool to New York being on 22 April 1893. She had quite an eventful history: she was the first ship to be fitted with Marconi's Wireless Telegraph system in 1901; in 1914 she was sold to the breaker's yard but before she could be broken up, she was bought by the Admiralty; they commissioned Cammell Laird of* **Birkenhead** *to convert her into an Aircraft Carrier and she became the first ship to launch an aircraft while in motion; she survived attacks from German U Boats but finally sank after colliding with HMS* Revenge *in the Firth of Forth in 1918*

Above: *This photograph of Lord Street in 1897 shows the portable extension ladder which was for use in case of fire - to the left of the ladder is a horse-drawn cart loaded with children - note also that all the men wore hats from bowlers to trilbys and even a top hat*

Queen Victoria's Diamond Jubilee Day. A procession through the city of Trades and Friendly Societies composed of some 15,000 people - there were 18 bands with magnificent banners; the Lord Mayor and Lady Mayoress gave a garden party at the Botanical Gardens with over 2,000 guests; at St George's Hall over 1,000 of the poor were entertained for dinner; in various parks old English games and amusements were arranged for the school children; at St Paul's Churchyard, the Mayor distributed Jubilee Medals to the children - who then marched to the landing stage where they embarked on several steamers to witness a marine display and in the evening there was a firework and electric light display from many of the steamers.

Above: The horse-drawn tram No.231, pulled by four horses, is seen heading towards the overhead railway from Pier Head

Left: This postcard was published to show the birthplace of the Prime Minister, Mr Gladstone, he died at Hawarden 19 May 1898

Feb 2	**Crosby** Lighthouse burnt in which the keeper, his wife and one other lost their lives
Feb 15	The brewer TW Thorougood Ltd, **Waterloo** changed its name to Thorougoods Breweries Ltd[WHATBG]
Mar 15	*Blundell Arms* ph. **Hightown** - sold £3,500[LCPS]
Apr 1	New Horse Bus service **Aigburth** (Lark Lane) - Breckfield Road South[LTVol2]
Apr 23	**Crosby** Lightship sunk by the SS *Mediana*
May 19	The Prime Minister, Wm. Gladstone, who was born at 62, Rodney Street, died at Hawarden (*see photo*)
June 22	Construction of experimental electric tramway commenced from St George's Church to the **Dingle**
Sept 23	The Port Guardship Squadron arrived in the Mersey comprising the following ships: *Nile, Thunderer, Sanspariel, Trafalgar* and *Spanker*
Sept 26	600 Bluejackets and Marines from the squadron were entertained to dinner at St George's Hall and afterwards to the *Empire Theatre*
Nov 14	Liverpool Electric Tramways formally inaugurated
Nov 16	First Electric Tram service: **Dingle** to South Castle Street[LTVol2]
Dec 19	The Liverpool Athenaeum celebrated its centenary

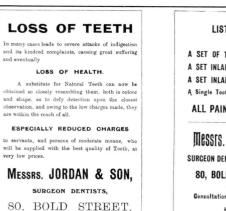

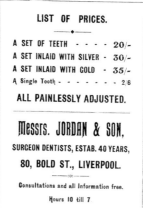

LOSS OF TEETH

In many cases leads to severe attacks of indigestion and its kindred complaints, causing great suffering and eventually

LOSS OF HEALTH.

A substitute for Natural Teeth can now be obtained so closely resembling them, both in colour and shape, as to defy detection upon the closest observation, and owing to the low charges made, they are within the reach of all.

ESPECIALLY REDUCED CHARGES

to servants, and persons of moderate means, who will be supplied with the best quality of Teeth, at very low prices.

MESSRS. JORDAN & SON,

SURGEON DENTISTS,

80, BOLD STREET.

LIST OF PRICES.

A SET OF TEETH - - - - 20/-
A SET INLAID WITH SILVER - 30/-
A SET INLAID WITH GOLD - 35/-
A Single Tooth - - - - - - 2/6

ALL PAINLESSLY ADJUSTED.

Messrs. JORDAN & SON,

SURGEON DENTISTS, ESTAB. 40 YEARS,

80, BOLD ST., LIVERPOOL.

Consultations and all information free.

Hours 10 till 7

*Below: This odd looking German 'Altona' Tramcar No.414 on Route 'A' to **Dingle** is pictured at South Castle Street. This car was one of 15 sets of trams ordered for Liverpool - they were the first electric trams in the town - each tram had a trailer - and were replaced with conventional trams in 1901*

1899

Jan 12   School for the blind opened at **Wavertree**

Feb 2   Liverpool School of Commerce and the Victoria University formerly opened

Apr 8   The foundation stone laid for Ogden's new tobacco factory off West Derby Road[LDPCE]

May 15   Auction - *The Freshfield Hotel* **Freshfield** - sold £3,650[LCPS]

June 23   Liverpool Stock Exchange new buildings opened

July 19   HRH Duke of York officially opened the New General Post Office in Victoria Street

July 26   The Catholic reform ship *Clarence*, lying in the Sloyne, was burnt out - 235 officers and boys rescued

Aug 3   Royal Lancashire Agricultural Show held on 44 acres of the **Wavertree** playground - the avenues were over 25 miles in total

Aug 3   Inauguration of a direct shipping line from Liverpool to Australia - when the White Star liner *Medic* began the first of a monthly service

Sept 6   Maiden voyage of the White Star liner *Oceanic (II)* from Liverpool to New York (*see photo*)

Sept 20   *Coach & Horses* ph. + 2 shops Scotland Road - sold £3,400[LCPS]

Oct 15   New Post Office in Victoria Street opened for business

Nov 23   Thomas Ismay died - head of the White Star Line

Nov 27   Memorial Service held at St Nicholas' Church for Thomas Ismay - followed by buriel at **Thurstaston**

Dec 17   Omnibus service between Smithdown Road & Pier Head withdrawn[LTVol2]

Above: The White Star Liner Oceanic (II) *is seen berthed at Riverside Station, Liverpool - her maiden voyage from Liverpool to New York was on 6 September 1899*

Above: Thorougood's Breweries Ltd, Lion Brewery (pictured top left in Advert) was built in **Waterloo** *1877/8 by William Okell of the Falcon Brewery, Douglas, Isle of Man to introduce his popular Light India Ale to the mainland. TW Thorougood was registered in June 1896 and the name was changed to Thorougood's Breweries Ltd on 15 February 1898. The brewery was taken over by Threllfalls Brewery Co Ltd in 1925[WHATBG]*

Feb 4	St Saviour's Church, Upper Parliament Street, destroyed by fire
Feb 22	New wing for outpatients at Stanley Hospital was opened by the Mayor
Mar 24	Rev FJ Chavasse was appointed as Bishop of Liverpool
Apr 23	The Gladstone Conservatory was erected in **Stanley** Park
Apr 25	Rev Francis James Chavasse consecrated by the Bishop of Liverpool at York Cathedral
May	Auction - Smithy and 3 houses Mill Road **Everton** - sold £800[LCPS]
June 20	Liverpool Overhead Railway Tramway opened **Seaforth** Sands to St Georges Road **Waterloo**[LTVol2]
July 8	Fire occurred at West Toxteth Dock - £16,000 damage
July 19	Pier Head terminus opened for electric trams[LTVol2]
July 31	George's Dock closed
Sept 8	Auction - Dairy + house 1-3 The Green, London Road - sold £910[LCPS]
Sept 12	Auction - 'Chesterfield Farm' Chesterfield Road, Great **Crosby** - sold £2,960[LCPS]
Sept 18	Royal National Eisteddfod held at Liverpool for 4 days
Sept 27	New **Bootle** Technical School opened - cost £22,000
Oct 23	*Queen's Arms* Public House Corner Admiral Street & South Street withdrawn from auction - bid of £5,500 with £7,000 reserve[LCPS]
Nov 27	Liverpool welcomed three officers and 133 men of the 5th VB of the King's Liverpool Regiment, on their return home from the Boer War in South Africa - not one of the Company died in combat - they were entertained by the Mayor in St George's Hall
Dec 10	Canadian Volunteer troops stopped at Liverpool on their way home from the Boer War

Above: Joseph Booth, Wine Merchant, was established in Liverpool in 1851 (see 1952)

Left: Horse Tram No.167 was of the Eades patent design with stairs at only one end. The body of the car could be turned without unharnessing the horses just by removing a locking pin

Below: Crowds are queueing up for the paddle steamer, whilst horses & carts on the right are heading for the luggage boats on the floating landing stage

1901

Jan 18   The Victoria Cross conferred on Pte. William Heaton, 1st Battalion, King's Liverpool Regiment

Jan 22   **Queen Victoria died** - theatres closed, Church bells tolled, entertainments and meetings abandoned

Feb 2   Services held following the death of Queen Victoria

Feb 4   Weight of snow brought down telephone wires near the Royal Infirmary which came into contact with tram wires causing a powerful voltage - killed two people

Feb 23   On their way home from the Boer War, "Strathcona's Horse" were officially welcomed at St George's Hall by the Lord Mayor

Mar 15   A new ward at the Stanley Hospital opened by the Lord Mayor

Mar 29   *Nelson Arms* bh. St Marys Road **Garston** - sold £2,500[LCPS]

Mar 30   About 400 Bluejackets, attached to a flotilla of Torpedo Destroyers, entertained by the Mayor

Census: The population of Liverpool and the suburbs (including the extended area to the city boundaries in 1895) was 681,947 - an increase of 55,399 since 1891

May   Liverpool FC 1st Division League Champions 1900/01

May 8   Allerton House, **Allerton** Road, sold at auction for £10,000[LCPS]

May 18   The Service Company of the King's Liverpool Regiment returned from the Boer War to an enthusiastic reception

July 23   Auction - *The Prince of Wales Theatre* Clayton Square - withdrawn at £13,000 - reserve £20,000[LCPS]

July 25   Auction - 'Broadgreen Hall', Broadgreen Road - sold £6,300[LCPS]

July 26   The world's largest steamer - the *Celtic* left Liverpool on her maiden voyage (*see photo*)

July 26   The statue of William Rathbone was unveiled in St John's Gardens

Oct 8   Lord Roberts of Candahar and Pretoria presented medals to about 600 men, who had taken part in the Boer War, in front of St George's Hall

Oct 26   The Municipal Central Technical School opened in Bryom Street

Oct 29   High class concerts given at **Knotty Ash** Village Hall

Dec 23   An electrical fault on a train on the Overhead Railway caused a fire which killed six passengers

Above: Described at the time as the world's largest steamer - the White Star Line Celtic left Liverpool 26 July 1901 on her maiden voyage to New York. She survived the First World War, became stranded on rocks off Queenstown 1928 and was a total loss - finally dismantled in 1933[WS]

Above: Richmond Fair or Richmond Woollen Hall was one of Liverpool's oldest parts dating back to 1787 when the buildings were erected as a mart for the sale of Yorkshire woollen goods - some dealers were permanent and others attended the quarterly fairs. Initially business was good but eventually trade dropped off and the premises became occupied by washerwomen[MOL]

Below: The railway engines operating on the Euston to Liverpool Riverside Station were too heavy for the bridge over Prince's Dock so tank engines, like the one pictured Liverpool, were used from Edge Hill to Riverside

- Marsh Lane, **Bootle**, open-air baths opened - later covered in (*see 1927*)[BOH]
- Ogden's became part of The Imperial Tobacco Company (*see article this page*)[LDPCE]

Mar 13   The David Lewis Northern Hospital opened - cost over £100,000 (*see photo*)[LNH]

Mar 19   *Coach & Horses* ph. + house etc, 21-29 Woolton Street **Woolton** - sold £1,850[LCPS]

May 15   **Newsham** Park Aviary opened

June   Auction - 'The Calderstones Estate', Calderstones Road **Allerton** - sold £43,000[LCPS]

June 1   **End of the Boer War** announced by The Lord Mayor

Jun 5   Auction - *Sun Inn* ph. + shop Redcross Street - sold £900[LCPS]

June 25   **Old Swan** Tramway extended to **Knotty Ash** linking with the Lancashire Light Railways Co Ltd Knotty Ash – St Helens line, opened same day[LTVol2]

July 8   The 2nd Service Company of the King's Liverpool Regiment arrived home from South Africa

Aug 8   **Coronation of Edward VII** - The city was elaborately decorated and following a procession to the Cathedral Church of St Peter during the day, firework displays were held in the evening at **Sefton** and Newsham Parks

Aug 28   Last Horse Bus withdrawn (**Aigburth** Vale to **Garston**)[LTVol2]

Sept 18   Auction - *The Shakespeare Theatre* built 1896, 4-8 Fraser Street - sold £4,750[LCPS]

Oct 15   **Toxteth** branch Library opened - cost over £12,000

Oct 15 -   Smithy and house 42 Taylor Street (off Scotland Road) sold £480[LCPS]

Nov 8   City boundary extended to include **Garston**

Dec 6   Last horse car in city of Liverpool ran on Outer Circle on which electric cars were already running[LTVol2]

Above: Liverpool Corporation Standard Open-top Tram No.387 in Islington where the shops are decorated with flags on King Edward VII's Coronation Day 8 August 1902 and the tram's passengers are all in festive mood

Thomas Ogden started as a tobacconist in Park Lane, Liverpool in 1860 and commenced manufacturing in St James Street in 1866. He acquired further premises in Cornwallis Street in 1870 and expanded further in 1890 when six factories and stores were acquired - it then became a Private Limited Company. The foundation stone for a new factory, off West Derby Road, was laid 18 April 1899 - when completed all the company's manufacturing interests were housed under one roof

The David Lewis Northern Hospital opened 13 March 1902 - built at a cost of over £100,000 it was funded by the David Lewis Trust which was set up by his nephew, Mr BW Levy, with money left after David Lewis's death in 1885. When it opened it was described as being the finest hospital in the country with 225 beds, a splendidly equipped operating theatre,a room devoted to the treatment of lupus by Finsen light, a Turkish Bath and a separate out-patient department. The fact that few major alterations were made over the years speaks well of the original plan. During the Second World War the hospital was taken over by the Royal Navy and the wards moved to St Katherine's College, Childwall, returning in 1947 (see 1947)

Above: Two pictures of the North Western Hotel, *Lime Street showing the Dining Room and Vestibule - they were sold as postcards and posted in 1902*

Right: Liverpool Overhead Railway **Crosby** *Tram decorated for the Coronation of King Edward VII with Jack Grimster the driver*

Above: The horses and carriage are waiting outside the main entrance to Newsham House, Newsham Park, to transport a Judge, who is seen on the steps. Newsham House was purchased by Liverpool Corporation for £80,000 in 1868. On her last visit to Liverpool in 1886, Queen Victoria stayed here. This was used as the Judges' Lodgings and still is today

Right: White Star liner Cedric, *then the largest ship in the world, launched 21 August 1902, she is seen at Princes Landing Stage - sailed on her maiden voyage - Liverpool to New York on 11 February 1903*

Above: Liverpool Corporation Tramcar No. 472 is seen outside **Walton** *Tram depot when new in 1902 - the temporary top cover was replaced with a permanent one in 1903 - this tram was in service until 1937*

Feb 11 White Star liner *Cedric*, the largest ship in the world, sailed on her maiden voyage - Liverpool to New York (*see photo opposite*)

Feb 19 Auction - *Greyhound Hotel* ph. 27 Prescot Road **Knotty Ash** - sold £10,050[LCPS]

Mar 5 Auction - 'The Old Police Station' Bridge Road **Seaforth** - sold £640[LCPS]

Mar 30 A convoy of trams ran from the Pier Head to Bolton - to demonstrate the possibility of through services for both passengers and goods

Apr *Railway Hotel* + 'Roscoe Chambers' offices 20-22 Tithebarn Street - sold £21,000[LCPS]

Apr 6 *Cart & Horses* ph. stabling + lock-up shop 20-24 Vauxhall Road - sold £2,400[LCPS]

May 3 Mersey Railway operated their first electric tram

May 18 An electric tram service established between Liverpool Pier Head and **St Helens** via **Knotty Ash**

June 12 Auction - *The Central Hotel*, 29-31 Ranelagh Street - sold £11,300[LCPS]

June 26 White Star liner *Arabic* left Liverpool on her maiden voyage to New York

July 15 Disaster on the Lancashire & Yorkshire Railway at **Waterloo** Station when an engine was derailed and mounted the platform - eight people killed (*see photo*)

July 15 A Charter of Incorporation was granted, constituting Liverpool the seat of a separate University - to be known as the University of Liverpool

July 16 Beech Lodge, Allerton Road, **Allerton** with 2.25 acres of land sold at auction for £2,500[LCPS]

Aug 4 HM Government made public the agreement by which they acquired a control over the steamships of the Cunard Company

Aug 25 Horse car withdrawn between **Linacre** and **Litherland** (last horse car to run in Liverpool district)[LTVol2]

Oct 1 The Dominion liner *Colombus* sailed from Liverpool on her maiden voyage to Boston

Oct 8 Mersey Docks & Harbour Board purchased **Seaforth** Hall Estate for dock extension

Nov 4 Foundation stone for a block of municipal dwellings to accommodate 2,236 people was laid by HRH Princess Louise

Nov 7 The inauguration of the University of Liverpool at St George's Hall

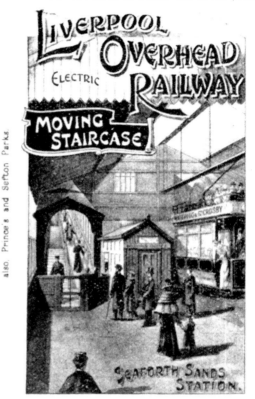

Above Top : *An advert for the Liverpool Overhead Railway including the moving staircase at* **Seaforth** *Sands Station*

Above: *Disaster on the Lancashire & Yorkshire Railway at* **Waterloo** *Station when an engine was derailed and mounted the platform - eight people were killed*

Left: *The Globe Express Ltd advertised as 'City & Suburban Carriers 11 North John Street & 4 Wood Street'*

Above: Royal Hotel *(the tall building on the right), Marine Terrace,* **Waterloo** *- originally called the* Royal Waterloo Hotel *- probably named after the Battle of Waterloo - an 1816 map calls it the* Waterloo Hotel *- it changed its name by dropping the 'Waterloo' part c1875 and became the* Royal Hotel. *However, the name Waterloo still remains today*

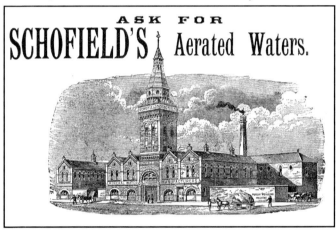
Below: *St Peter's Church was the first church to be built by the Corporation in 1704 following the Parish of Liverpool being created - it became a Catholic Church in 1880 and was demolished in 1922 - Church Street is named after it*

*The Village Stocks at **West Derby** were enclosed
and a plaque placed there inscribed:-*
'To commemorate the long and happy reign of
Queen Victoria and the Coronation of King Edward VII
this site of the ancient Pound of the Dukes of
Lancaster and others Lords of the Manor of West Derby
was enclosed and planted and the Village Stocks
set herein Easter 1904'

•	Stanley Ornamental Garden opened in **Bootle**
Mar 30	The Liverpool Corporation's new storage reservoir opened at **Prescot** by Lady Derby - capacity of 121 million gallons
Easter	Village Stocks at **West Derby** enclosed in memory of Queen Victoria's reign and Edward VII's Coronation (*see photo*)
Apr 2	The Church of the Good Shepherd **West Derby**, consecrated
Apr 5	The Lancashire & Yorkshire Railway Co's electric train service opened between Liverpool and **Southport**
Apr 13	**Bootle** Fire Station opened - cost £32,000
June 29	White Star Liner *Baltic*, the largest steamship in the world, sailed on her maiden voyage to New York
June 29	St John's Gardens, adjoining St George's Hall, opened to the public - cost £24,000
July 16	The statue of William Gladstone unveiled in St John's Gardens - cost £5,000
July 19	The King and Queen laid the foundation stone for the Anglican Cathedral
July 21	Statue of Sir Bower Forwood, Bart, unveiled in St John's Gardens
July 25	Auction - Oakvale Nursery, Broadgreen Road **Broadgreen** sold £6,550[LCPS]
Aug 25	The Allan liner *Victorian* launched - the first steamer for the Atlantic trade with turbines
Oct 26	Auction - *Grapes Hotel* ph. 25 Mathew Street - sold £2,700[LCPS]
Nov 12	New Medical School and the George Holt Physics Laboratory opened at Liverpool University
Nov 14	The *Liverpool Mercury* and the *Liverpool Daily Post* amalgamated and published for the first time as the *Liverpool Daily Post and Liverpool Mercury*
Dec 14	The School of Veterinary Medicine and Surgery opened at Liverpool University
Dec 22	New Hospital for Consumption and Diseases of the Chest opened at Mount Pleasant

*Left: Lewis's departmental store in Ranelagh
Street decorated for the visit of the King in 1904*

*Below: The Royal Yacht is seen at the Liverpool landing stage
berthed next to a paddle steamer*

Above: Looking up London Road - Tram No.173 built in 1900 by Dick Kerr with 56 seats - pictured here with an open top which was covered in 1904 and was withdrawn from service in 1936. The Legs of Man *pub is pictured on the right and Crawford's Umbrella, Parasol and Stick Manufacturer on the left corner*

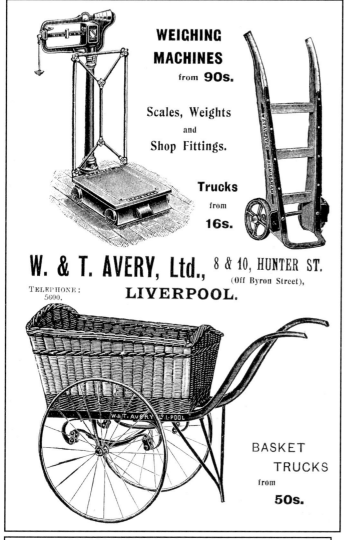

WEIGHING MACHINES from **90s.**

Scales, Weights and Shop Fittings.

Trucks from **16s.**

W. & T. AVERY, Ltd., 8 & 10, HUNTER ST. (Off Byron Street), **LIVERPOOL.**

TELEPHONE: 5600.

BASKET TRUCKS from **50s.**

EVERYONE IS WAKING UP TO THE FACT

That the best place to buy . . Brushes is from **THE PERFECT BRUSH COY., L**TD. 106, WHITECHAPEL, Telephone No. 7016. *Liverpool.*

TOILET BRUSHES, the best value, best selection.

House Brushes, Stable Brushes, Printers' Brushes of every description.

J. WHITEHURST STORER, Managing Director.

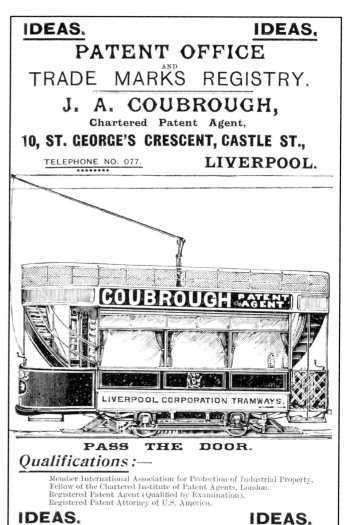

Above: These trams are heading to and from the landing stage before June 1904 when the tram on the left No.170 had its top covered - note the horse cabs waiting in line on the left

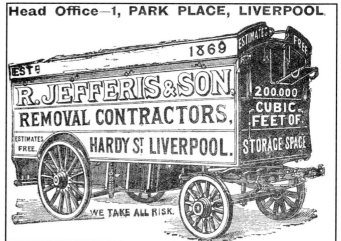

Feb 25   Cunard liner *Caronia's* maiden voyage to New York

Apr 10   Welsh Presbyterian Church opened at Breeze Hill

Apr 24   The *Olympia Theatre* opened in West Derby Road (*see photo*)

Apr 28   Robbery of Nelson relics at Liverpool Museum

June 26   Maiden voyage of the turbine steamer *Viking* to Douglas, Isle of Man

June 27   Green Lane Branch Library opened in **West Derby** - cost of £15,750 paid for by Andrew Carnegie

July 14   Presentation of Colours to the 3rd and 4th Battalions of the Kings Own Royal Lancaster Regiment by His Majesty the King

July 27   Accident at Hall Road station on the Liverpool and **Southport** line of the Lancashire and Yorkshire Railway - 20 people killed

Aug 21   Opening of the Aviary at the Botanic Gardens

Sept 9   Boer War Statue unveiled in St John's Gardens (*see picture*)

Oct 16   The second pipe of the Vyrnwy Water Supply opened

Nov 9   Amalgamation of **Orrell** with **Bootle**

Nov 18   Opening of the New Museum and Laboratories of Zoology at Liverpool University

Dec 2   New Cunard turbine liner *Carmania* set off from Liverpool on her maiden voyage to New York

Dec 5   Liverpool Wesleyan Central (Charles Garrett) Memorial Hall opened

Dec 13   Auction - *Corn Market Hotel* and *Bull's Head* ph. 1 Old Ropery - sold £8,700[LCPS]

Below: King Edward VII & Queen in their carriage having laid the foundation stone for the Anglican Cathedral

Above: The Boer War Memorial, which was sculptured by Sir John W Goscombe, was unveiled in St John's Gardens on 9 September 1905. It shows Britannia on top of the pedestal with four soldiers at each corner representing a period in the history of the King's Regiment (Liverpool)

Left: The Olympia Theatre, *West Derby Road,* opened 24 April 1905. It was part of Moss Empires Ltd - then the largest variety theatre in Great Britain which could seat an audience of 3,750. Over the next 20 years it entertained as a circus; water pageant; opera; ballet; music hall; pantomime; showed films; boxing etc. In May 1916 it became a cinema and in 1925 was sold to Savoy Cinemas Ltd, re-opening 30 March 1925 as the Olympia Super Cinema *and in 1929 became the first cinema in Liverpool and the fourth outside London to be equipped for 'talkies'. In 1930 it was taken over by Associated British Cinemas Ltd but during the war became a naval depot and in 1948 sold to Mecca Ltd who converted it into the Locarno Ballroom*

1906

- Langton Dock Station closed on the Liverpool Overhead Railway[ISOLRS]
- **Orrell Park** Station opened on the Lancashire & Yorkshire Railway line[ISOLRS]

January The **Allerton** Estate, Allerton Road sold at auction for £50,000

Jan 12 Roby Hall Estate gifted to Liverpool by Alderman WR Bowring

Mar 13 Smithy + 17 houses 1-35 Wrexham Street **Kirkdale** - sold £3,500[LCPS]

Apr 25 New City Hospital opened at **Fazakerley**

May Liverpool FC 1st Division Champions 1905/06

May 29 The Picton Road Baths opened in **Wavertree**

June **Everton** FC winners of the FA Cup

June 1 Ford Station and Linacre Road Station opened on the Lancashire & Yorkshire Railway[ISOLRS]

June 8 Sir Thomas Brocklebank died at **Woolton**

June 12 Explosion aboard the SS *Haverford* at Huskisson Dock killed 12 people - many were injured

Sept 27 HRH Princess Louise unveiled the Queen Victoria Memorial (*see photo*)

Nov 30 New Cotton Exchange opened by TRH the Prince and Princess of Wales

Dec 8 Statue of Monsignor Nugent unveiled in St John's Gardens

Top: The Curator's House is seen in the Botanic Gardens

Above: Cunard Liner Mauretania *is seen at Liverpool Landing Stage - she was launched on 20 September 1906 and on 16 November 1907 sailed for New York on her maiden voyage - she was then the largest and fastest ship in the world - May 1915 she was converted to a Troop Ship at Gladstone Dock, Liverpool - in 1922 was changed from burning coal to oil and was scrapped in 1934*

Above: The original purpose-built Philharmonic Hall in Hope Street, seen here in 1906, was opened in 1849. It was burnt down in 1933 and replaced in 1939 with the present building (see 1939)

Right: The crowds are gathered for the unveiling of the Queen Victoria Memorial on 27 September 1906 by HRH Princess Louise

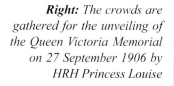

Jan 2   New Cotton Exchange opened for business

Jan 10   New Children's Infirmary opened in Myrtle Street

Apr 24   New organ at the Central Hall in place

Apr 24   Lancashire & Yorkshire Railway bus service commenced - **Thornton** to **Blundellsands** and **Crosby** station[LTVol2]

May 25 Hall and Sunday School opened in memory of Dr JH Lundie

June 12 Bowring Park opened - presented to the city by Alderman CT Bowring

July 10 Mark Twain entertained at a complimentary banquet by the Lord Mayor

July 12 Liverpool Institute Cadet Corps Rifle Range opened

July 15 Mersey Docks and Harbour Board new offices opened on the site of the Old George's Dock

Aug 3   Opening of the celebrations in honour of the 700th anniversary of the granting of a Royal Charter to Liverpool by King John in 1207 - a great pageant was held on the 3rd, 5th & 6th August (*See next page*)

Aug 22 Opening of the new Corporation Baths at **Garston**

Sept 7   Cunard liner *Lusitania* left Liverpool on her record-breaking maiden voyage to New York (*see photo*)

Nov   Shop (late *Quarry Inn*) 38 Quarry Street **Woolton** - sold £6,750[LCPS]

Nov 16 Cunard liner *Mauretania* left Liverpool on her maiden voyage to New York

Dec 11   Auction - *Swan Hotel* Carter Street **Toxteth Park** - sold £1,525[LCPS]

*Above: The driver and conductor of this **Woolton** Motor Omnibus Company's Durham Churchill charabanc, are posing with passengers - the weather must have been good as the canvas sides of the charabanc are rolled up - the sign board on top of the charabanc indicates 'Woolton & Brook House', a public house in Smithdown Road which still exists*

Right: This statue of Canon Major Lester is seen in St John's Memorial Gardens in 1907

Above: The Cunard liner Lusitania *is seen in the Mersey before setting out from Liverpool on her record-breaking maiden voyage to New York on 7 September 1907*

1907

The 700th Anniversary of Liverpool receiving her Charter in 1907 was celebrated in many ways

Right: The reverse side of this 700th Anniversary postcard says:- *This card is in commemoration of the Seventh Century of Liverpool, which was celebrated by a Great Historical Pageant on the 3rd, 5th & 6th August 1907, it being 700 years since the Charter of Liverpool was granted to the town by King John. The design inside the pillars represents the Liverpool Coat of Arms, but the two usual figures are changed to King Edward on the right and King John on the left*

The poem below the two men reads:

*No sooner were bolts
Of our liberty driven,
Than our City was Charter'd
Twelve Hundred and Seven.*

*Our freedom now won,
We wish peace to be given
To the world in the year
Nineteen hundred and seven*

Above: Tramcar No.4 at the Green Lane depot - decorated for the 700th Anniversary Liverpool Pageant

The 700th Anniversary Pageant was held in **Wavertree** Park and Grounds on August 3rd, 5th & 6th August 1907
Above:- *On top of The 'Grand Car of Liverpool' is a lady representing The City with a Liver Bird Sceptre in one hand - below her in front is a lady dressed as 'Rule Brittania' with the car being pulled by six horses in trappings of gold, led by Romans in togas and an escort either side of the tableau by men of the Royal Naval Reserve*

Below: *This tableau, which depicted the 'Slave Trade', being much smaller than the one above, only needed three horses to pull it*

The programme for the 700th Anniversary Festival included:- musical display by 2,000 Liverpool school children; an historical procession and tableaux, five military bands, choir of 1,000 voices in the Edge Lane Hall grounds, **Wavertree** Park; fireworks in **Sefton**, **Stanley** and **Newsham** Parks and a visit of the channel fleet of 14 battleships under the command of Admiral Lord Charles Beresford KCB, GCVO

Above: This was the scene following a collision in the Mersey between the Cunard liner RMS Etruria *and Mudhopper No.19*

Above: This postcard was of Greendale Road, **Walton**

Above: Edge Hill College opened in a large house in Durning Road, Liverpool and was the first non-denominational Teacher training college for women in the country. By 1925 it outgrew this site and was handed over to the Lancashire Education Committee. In 1931 the foundation stone was laid for its new home in **Ormskirk**

Jan 5	Centenary of the *Liverpool Courier*
Feb 6	New Carnegie Library opened at **Waterloo**
Mar 3	New hospital opened in Olive Mount
Apr 2	New **Blundellsands** Cottage Home erected at a cost of £1,280
June 3	New children's playground opened in Peel Road, **Bootle** - cost £2,700
June 23	Greenbank Estate, **Waterloo** opened - covered 18 acres and cost the Corporation £13,000 with a further £4,000 raised by public subscription
Aug 4	Centenary of the opening of the Liverpool Exchange
Aug 8	There was a collision in the Mersey between RMS *Etruria* and Mudhopper No.19 (*see photo*)
Sept 12	St David's Welsh Church, Merton Grove, **Bootle** consecrated
Oct 3	First 'Penny Postage' mail from Liverpool to the United States aboard the SS *Lusitania*
Oct 5	Emmanuel Church, **Fazakerley** consecrated - cost £10,000
Oct 20	The 14 acre South Dock opened at **Garston**
Dec 27	Church of St Mark, Upper Duke Street, closed due to small congregation - opened in 1803 and was the largest church in the Liverpool Diocese

Above: W&F Walker of Water Street, Liverpool, the manufacturers of 'Carbolacene', claimed that one cupful of their product in a bucket of water would 'save labour' and 'no need to use soaps or dangerous disinfectants'

Left: Horse-drawn carts and wagons are seen queueing on the floating landing stage for the luggage ferry to cross over the River Mersey to either Wallasey or Birkenhead - seen beyond the liner in the middle of the river. A paddle-steamer ferry boat is seen just off the landing stage. The floating landing stage was half a mile long and the longest in the world

1908

Right: Seamen's Orphanage, whose foundation stone was laid 11 September 1871, is seen in Orphan Drive beyond the church, taken from Newsham Drive in 1908

Above: The shop manager in the middle and two assistants who are wearing flat caps, are posing in front of this Blackledge's Bread shop which states 'largest sale in Liverpool & District' - the company dates back to 1849 with a shop in Fox Street (see also 1949)

Above: Howard's, manufacturers of tents and marquees also produced tarpaulins, nose bags, coal sacks and even temporary ballrooms with parquet flooring - all at their Denbigh Street works with their office and shop at 35 Redcross Street

Right: Tram No.126 on the left in Lord Street is open-topped with the other three enclosed. Bunney's departmental store is behind the second tram from the left

Feb 24 New **Garston** Dock built by the London & North Western Railway Company, opened by the chairman Lord Stalbridge

Apr 5 New Corporation Baths opened in Queens Drive **Walton**

Apr 19 White Star liner *Laurentic* left Liverpool on her maiden voyage to Quebec

July 5 Review of the West Lancashire Division of the Territorial forces at **Knowsley** Park by HRH The King

Sept 9 Cunard liner *Mauretania* beat the Trans-Atlantic crossing by 7 minutes - in 4 days, 11 hours, 35 minutes - beating her sister ship, *Lusitania's,* record

Oct 15 **Crosby** Lightship struck by a tug and sank

Nov 25 Mr SF Cody flew his aeroplane at **Aintree**

Dec 29 The 233 acre **Allerton** Cemetery opened - cost £55,000

*Above: **St Helen's** tramways car No.34 outside the Blue Bell Inn at **Huyton** on the Liverpool & Prescot line*

Left: Delegates to the 1909 Esperanto Conference in Liverpool are seen on St George's Hall steps

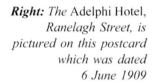

Right: The Adelphi Hotel, Ranelagh Street, is pictured on this postcard which was dated 6 June 1909

Left: This was a postcard sent from a member of the 6th King's Liverpool Regiment's Camp at Caerwys, North Wales in 1909. According to the message, some of the men were suffering - the message read:-"Dear Fred, Having a grand time. A good many in hospital. The hills about here are awful to climb. Home on Sunday, William".
The soldiers are not marching off on foot - but pushing bicycles!

*Above: This multi-view greetings postcard from **Gateacre** was posted in 1909 and shows the Wilson Memorial Fountain in the top picture; The Nook bottom left and the Post Office bottom the right*

C. SUNDERLAND

. . SHOWS ONE OF THE FINEST SELECTIONS OF . .

Real Harris, Skye, St. Kilda, Shetland, Highland Homespuns, And Genuine Scotch Cheviot Suitings in the Provinces.

Suit, to order only, from THREE GUINEAS.

18, NORTH JOHN STREET, LIVERPOOL.

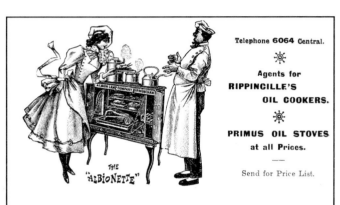

Telephone **6064** Central.

Agents for
**RIPPINCILLE'S
OIL COOKERS.**

PRIMUS OIL STOVES
at all Prices.

Send for Price List.

H. H. JORDAN & CO.

Ironmongers, Cutlers, Engravers, Electricians, &c.,

46 Whitechapel, Liverpool.

And at 35 **WILLIAMSON STREET.**

Right: This GWR Milnes Daimler bus offered a service between Birkenhead (Woodside) station and the principal hotels in Liverpool. It started 20 September 1909 but only lasted three months, being abandoned in December 1909

Right: Liverpool College was founded in 1840 when the foundation stone of this building was laid in Shaw Street Liverpool and Rev WJ Conybeare was appointed as Principal. The school, which opened in 1843, cost £36,000. There were three schools : Upper, Middle and Lower - within the first year there were over 430 boys. In 1907 the school moved to a site in Lodge Lane and sold these buildings to the Liverpool Corporation for £12,500 who opened their own school here, calling it the Liverpool Collegiate School.
*In 1924 Liverpool College bought a 10 acre site at **Mossley Hill** and in 1929 built the Junior School wing. Building restrictions were lifted after the War and from 1953 - the new dining hall, science labs etc were built*

Jan 9   Drill Hall opened at **Crosby** by Lord Derby

Jan 13   New Liverpool Dispensary in Richmond Row, opened by Lord Derby

May 6   King Edward VII died[LDPCE]

June 17 New schools in Christian Street opened - cost £13,000

June 18 Huge demonstration in support of Women's Suffrage held outside St George's Hall[VFW]

June 29 Consecration of the Lady Chapel at the Cathedral by the Bishop, Dr Chavasse (*see photo*)

Oct   Schooner *Creek Fisher* ashore at **Blundellsands** (*see photo*)

Nov 21   New out-patients department of the Royal Southern Hospital opened

Nov 26   Church of St David, Hampstead Road, consecrated

Nov 29   Mr C Compton Paterson flew across the Mersey and back accompanied by Mr RA King of Neston (*see photo*)

Above: This postcard was described as follows:- "Messrs Paterson and King starting from Freshfield Aerodrome for a flight to Hoylake Nov. 29 1910 - the very first occasion on which an aeroplane has crossed the Mersey carrying a passenger." Mr Compton Paterson was the owner of the Farman Biplane seen taking off from Freshfield sands which is where the aerodrome was based - both men were wearing lifebelts in case the machine came down in the River Mersey

Above: This view from St James' Cemetery shows the main part of the new Liverpool Cathedral in the process of being built, with the completed Lady Chapel behind

Above: This parade of clergy is passing through an armed guard on their way to the consecration of the Lady Chapel at Liverpool Cathedral 29 June 1909 by Bishop, Dr Chavasse

Above: A crowd is standing by the three-masted schooner, the *Creek Fisher*, built in 1890 for James Fisher & son of Barrow, which is seen beached off **Blundellsands** - her sister ship *Lucy Bain* suffered the same fate some years earlier

Above: Liverpool College for Girls at **Huyton** was a complex of Victorian villas previously owned by merchants and ship owners which became collectively the sister school to Liverpool College. The main building for the girls' school, which opened in 1894, was The Orchard (seen here). At the time of this picture, there was a Headmistress and eight Assistant Mistresses. During World War Two, the girls were evacuated to a house called Blackwell in Bowness, Cumbria, returning in 1947. The school later became Huyton College but closed down in 1993 - its 99th year

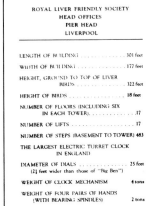

ROYAL LIVER FRIENDLY SOCIETY HEAD OFFICES PIER HEAD LIVERPOOL	
LENGTH OF BUILDING	301 feet
WIDTH OF BUILDING	177 feet
HEIGHT, GROUND TO TOP OF LIVER BIRDS	322 feet
HEIGHT OF BIRDS	18 feet
NUMBER OF FLOORS (INCLUDING SIX IN EACH TOWER)	17
NUMBER OF LIFTS	17
NUMBER OF STEPS (BASEMENT TO TOWER)	483
THE LARGEST ELECTRIC TURRET CLOCK IN ENGLAND	
DIAMETER OF DIALS (2½ feet wider than those of "Big Ben")	25 feet
WEIGHT OF CLOCK MECHANISM	4 tons
WEIGHT OF FOUR PAIRS OF HANDS (WITH BEARING SPINDLES)	2 tons

Above: a postcard giving the dimensions of the Royal Liver Building, which was opened in 1910 and included the famous two Liver birds, which stood 18 ft. tall.
Below: an advertising postcard for the builders of the clock, Gent & Co of Leicester, who described the "Great George", as being the largest electric clock in the world

"GREAT GEORGE" LIVERPOOL. The Largest Electric Clock in the World. DESIGNED, MANUFACTURED AND ERECTED BY GENT & CO. LTD, LEICESTER.

Above: Tram No.249 on the right is seen in London Road - the statue of George III in the background in Monument Place was a bronze equestrian figure in Roman dress, erected in 1822

Above: This was the terminus for the Liverpool Overhead Railway Tramway at Victoria Road, **Great Crosby**. The line was officially opened on 19 June 1900, initially running as far as the Five Lamps, **Waterloo** - the whole line opened October 1900. This was the only independent electric tram system running from Liverpool - it survived until 31 December 1925 when the Waterloo & Crosby Motor Services Ltd operated a bus service instead which lasted until January 1931 then the company was taken over by Ribble Motor Services Ltd

Above: Opening of the Wesleyan Chapel in **West Derby**

May 1 Consecration of the Church of SS John and James **Litherland**

Census: Population of Liverpool and suburbs 746,566 (an increase of 42,000 since 1901)

May 30 Mr Henry G Melly flew an aeroplane around the city and across the river in 41 minutes

June 21 Coronation celebrations started - Lady Mayoress distributed gifts to St Paul's Eye Hospital, David Lewis Northern Hospital & Stanley Hospital – Treat for 1,300 Crippled & Invalided Children in Calderstones Park

June 22 Coronation of King George V - Sports and entertainments in the following parks:- **Stanley**; **Sefton**, **Newsham**; **Wavertree**; **Calderstones**; **Springfield** and **Knotty Ash**. Also Wavertree Playground; **Garston** and **Kirkdale** Recreation Grounds[LDPCE]

July 7 Mr Henry G Melly flew a monoplane to Manchester in 49 minutes and back in 65 minutes

Aug 3 Mr Andrew Carnegie opened the new library in **Sefton Park** and was subsequently enrolled as an Honorary Freeman of the City in recognition of his gift of four libraries and three reading rooms

Aug 8 Liverpool Strike started by railway workers

Aug 10 Proclamation by the Lord Mayor, warning the railway strikers that if necessary he would call out the military and exercise full powers under the Riot Act. Arrival of additional police from Leeds and Birmingham and 200 members of the Royal Irish Constabulary

Aug 11 Fifty tons of provisions conveyed from Brunswick Dock Station by men of the Royal Warwickshire Regiment and 250 police.
Riot Act read and mass meeting of the strikers on St George's Plateau dispersed by police - 12 policemen and over 100 strikers being injured. At night barricades were erected by the mob in Christian Street, when the military were summoned and the Riot Act was read again (*see photos on page 51*)

Aug 12 Three hundred tons of provisions etc conveyed by detachments of the Royal Scots Greys and Police from the **Edge Hill** Goods Station

Aug 16 Riot in Vauxhall Road - two people shot and several policemen injured[LDPCE]

Aug 22 Strike over - railway men resumed work

Oct 3 Memorial to the 16th Earl of Derby unveiled in St George's Hall

Nov 11 The *Liverpool Repertory Theatre* opened - later named the *Playhouse*

Nov 24 Explosion at J Bibby & Co's Oil Cake Mills, Great Howard Street, followed by fire - 36 people killed and 100 seriously injured

Above: *The old oak in Calderstones Park was said to be over 1,000 years old and believed to have been used as a meeting place for the Hundred Court of **Allerton**[POIOM]*

Above: *Liverpool Corporation Tramways car No.544 decorated for the Coronation of King George V - 22 June 1911. This was destined to be the last open balcony car, running until 1950*

*This advertising postcard for Cooper & Co's Stores claims they were "The largest in Liverpool - we pay carriage on all general orders, irrespective of amount" [they delivered to all areas of Liverpool at least once a day and some like **Everton** twice a day!]. Cooper's store pictured was situated on the corner of Church Street and Paradise Street. They were described as Tea and Coffee Merchants; Grocery, Provision Merchants; Manufacturers and Importers with factories and warehouses in Glasgow; branches in London, Scotland and North of England. The lasting impression of their stores was the wonderful aromas - especially the freshly-ground coffee*

Left: *This Liverpool Corporation tram pictured, is also bedecked with flags for the Coronation of King George V - the sign on the top deck indicates: **Garston**, Church Street, Pier Head. Liverpool Corporation took over Garston & District Tramways Company with the line opening 28 August 1902*

GE MILLS, CARBONORA - Photographers

This photographic company was founded in Liverpool by Gwilym Eiriol Mills c1908. He had moved with his family from their home in Llandiloes in Wales at the turn of the century, where his father, Thomas, had set up in 1876 as a portrait photographer in Garth, Bangor. Gwilym worked for a photographic company called Weisker Bros., 'Kinematograph & Photographic experts' in Wilde Street, Liverpool, off London Road and then bought the business. The company name came from the 'carbon' process used in developing and adding 'ora' onto the end ie 'Carbonora'. One of ten children, Gwilym was joined in the business by two of his brothers, Dorando and Jack, and sister Inez. Probably because their premises backed onto the stage-door of the Shakespeare Theatre, in December 1908 he gained the contract to photograph the cast of its pantomime and also that of the Royal Court - the postcards being sold in their foyers. Gwilym, himself, appeared on stage as an impersonator, winning 'talent night' competitions.

The earliest record of a 'Carbonora' postcard was at Leasowe in August 1908 - with many more photographs taken and postcards sold there over the next 10 years. Business must have been good and despite there being 115 photographers listed in the 1909 Kelly's Directory, GE Mills became the official photographer to the Liverpool Police Force and took the photographs for the 1911 Liverpool strike - they produced 80 postcards of the event (*see photos*). However, four of the numbered postcards were censored by the police, never sold and the originals destroyed. The company also took photographs of the police passing-out parades; various territorials 'at camp', studio portraits etc.

Being the eldest son, Gwilym, had been 'reserved' for home service during the First World War and was able to keep the business going. After the War, the two brothers who had worked for him, Dorando and Jack set up business on their own - trading as 'Mills Studios' and 'Dorondo Mills Studios'. Later, his sister Inez also set up her own studio, in Anfield Road, **Anfield** and after WWII in Rice Lane.

After the First World War Gwilym also opened a studio in Walton Road and was the official photographer for the Liverpool Football Club *(see 1928)*.

During the Second World War, most of the family were evacuated to Windermere and after their premises in the centre of Liverpool had been bombed during the 'May Blitz', with most of their records lost - Gwilym joined his family in the Lake District. He operated the **Walton** studio and also opened one in the High Street, Windermere where his son, John, helped in the school holidays. Their main business then was photographing young men in uniform before they went off to do their duty. John joined the company in 1950 and the studio was re-equipped following a decision to concentrate on commercial, aerial and industrial photography. The company purchased premises in Hope Street in 1960 and is still operating successfully today, having moved to larger premises the Wirral side of the Mersey as 'Mills Media', with John's son Andrew at the helm and one of his daughters, Jenny, as Financial Director - they are the fourth generation of the Mills family.

This May Day gathering which took place in front of St George's Hall 1911 - [photographer GE Mills, Carbonora - see article]

THE LIVERPOOL STRIKE OF 1911

The Liverpool Strike of 1911 can be traced back to the seamen's strike in June of that year. They wanted an increase in the basic wage of £4.50 a month, an end to degrading medical inspections, and their unions recognised. The seamen gained most of their demands and there followed massive recruitment into other unions.

Encouraged by the success of the seamen, other groups of workers decided to follow their example by going on strike in support of their own claims including railway workers from the Lancashire and Yorkshire North Docks depot in Liverpool and by 8 August the entire docks rail traffic was at a standstill.

The decision to call in extra police and the military was made on 9 August and Carbonora, being the official police photographers, took photographs of the action which were sold to newspapers and also made into postcards, selling the following day (see this page). *There were 80 numbered postcards in this series but four numbers were missing - they had been censored by the police and the negatives destroyed.*

On 17 August the Government intervened and two days later the railway companies capitulated. The strike was over and on 22 August the railwaymen resumed work. None of the Liverpool policemen who went on strike were re-instated and those who did not strike received a 'loyalty' payment.

Above: The vast crowds that assembled in front of St George's Plateau have isolated the two trams on the right. The 'blue collar' workers have flat caps, stewards and 'white collar' workers wore bowler hats or boaters
[photographer GE Mills, Carbonora]

Above: A fire has been started in Cavendish Street probably as a protest against the Civil Authorities who brought in an extra 2,000 troops following events on 'Bloody Sunday'
[photographer GE Mills, Carbonora]

*Above: Troops of the 18th Hussars, who are camped at **Edge Hill** Estate, are seen grooming their horses*
[photographer GE Mills, Carbonora]

Above: Taken at the junction of Hopwood Street and Vauxhall Road, 'X' marks the spot where a dock worker, Michael Prendegast, was one of two men shot dead by troops escorting police vans to Walton Gaol. They were attacked by a mob and and in clearing the streets two men were killed. This staged photograph shows local men reading the newspaper article about the killing (see picture above)
[photographer GE Mills, Carbonora]

Above: Horse-drawn police vans being escorted along County Road, Walton, by the Scots Greys - on their way to Walton Gaol
[photographer GE Mills, Carbonora]

Above: The White Star liner Olympic, *sister ship to the fated* Titanic, *launched 20 October 1910, is pictured in the Mersey*
[photographer GE Mills, Carbonora]

Above: Baker's Shore Cottage is seen perched on top of a cliff following a storm, which partly demolished the wall on the beach where the lady is standing. A writer conveyed his thoughts in 1910: "we tremble for the safety of this little cottage on the verge of the crumbling cliffs" *THotRaAPoTL*

Above: These children photographed in Poplar Bank **Huyton**, don't know whether to look at the photographer or to see who is inside the horse-drawn carriage

Above: Henry Melley is seen standing by his Bleirot monoplane on a visit to Freshfield's 'Airport', which was situated on the firm sands of **Freshfield's** shore. These 'seaside airports' were ideal for the pioneer aviators as they ensured a relatively soft landing on sand when they inevitably crashed

Feb 27   St Paul's Eye Hospital, Old Hall Street, opened - rebuilt at a cost of £17,760

Apr 14   Loss of the White Star liner *Titanic* on her maiden voyage from Southampton - total deaths *1,195* (*see photo of newsagent on next page*)

May 7   Gift to Liverpool University of a complete plant for wireless telegraphy by Sir William Hartley

June 14   New Corporation workmen's dwellings in the **Bevington** area, opened by the Lady Mayoress

Nov 6   Shipping service between Liverpool and Iceland instituted

Above: Blackler's Stores, pictured on the corner of Elliot Street and Great Charlotte Street, was founded in 1908 by Richard Blackler and AB Wallis. It was destroyed in the May Blitz of 1941 - the new store opened in 1953 - it closed in 1988

Above: The upstairs passengers on this bus, pictured in Cromptons Lane, face the front instead of the side and are open to the weather - as is the driver to a lesser extent, whose only protection from the elements is the flat roof

Above: Derby Road, **Huyton** Looking North (compare with 1948)

Above: This comic postcard shows a view of a ship at the Landing Stage and underneath a man with his arm around a young lady with the caption:
'Liverpool agrees with me splendidly, the people here vie one with the other - I'm giving one a really good time'.

Right:- This postcard shows the Cunard liner *Lusitania being loaded in Liverpool ready for a trip across to New York*

Above: Exchange Station, pictured on the left, was the terminus in Liverpool for the Lancashire & Yorkshire Railway Company

Above: This picture of Sefton Park Bandstand was a postcard sent in 1912 - situated in the centre of the lake it was an octagonal structure with slender iron columns and a pagoda roof with ornamental weather vane on top

Above: This view of the 'Bridge House' newsagent's shop at 40 Penny Lane was taken in May 1912 and is interesting for the newspaper bill boards which describe the horror of the sinking of the Titanic - with headlines such as:- "The Titanic Sinks"; "Titanic Sunk - 1684 Drowned"; "Titanic Founders with 1,600 Souls" etc

Jan	Construction of the Cunard Building, Pier Head commenced - partly on the site of the old George's Dock
Jan 7	Memorial unveiled at St Faith's Church, **Great Crosby** to Mr Joseph Bell, Chief Engineer of the ill-fated White Star liner *Titanic*
Jan 9	Collision in the Mersey between the Booth liner *Ambrose*, the Corporation hopper barge *Beta* and the Hoylake trawler *Fleetwing* - both the latter sank and 12 lives were lost
May 22	New Lightship placed at the Bar - 40,000 candle power (probably the most powerful lightship in existence)
June 24	New buildings and grounds for Merchant Taylor's School for Girls, **Great Crosby** dedicated by the Bishop of Liverpool
July 5	Six days before the King and Queen visited Liverpool, a home-made bomb exploded near the Town hall but caused little damage - it was thought it could have been the work of the Women's Suffrage Movement although none of their literature was found at the site (*see July 8*)
July 8	Lord Leverhulme's house at Rivington Pike was burnt down - the following day Mrs Edith Rigby, wife of a well respected Doctor, walked into a Liverpool Police Station and confessed to placing the bomb in Liverpool on 5 July and to the burning down of Lord Leverhulme's summer house at Rivington Pike
July 11	HRH King George V and Queen Mary opened the new Gladstone Dock at **Seaforth**. Some 60,000 children assembled at Everton FC ground of whom 15,000 gave a display of Swedish drill to the King and Queen
Sept 23	Seafield House, **Seaforth** destroyed by fire - estimated damage £80,000 - attributed to the Suffragettes
Oct	White Star liner *Lusitania* first ship to use the new Gladstone Dock
Oct 1	New Armour building opened at Merchant Taylor's School, **Great Crosby**, by the former headmaster, Canon Armour, after whom it was named
Nov	Demolition of St Mark's Church, Upper Duke Street
Nov 27	Cunard lines *Alaunia* left on her maiden voyage to Canada
Dec 5	Police Court opened at **Woolton**
Dec 6	New Reservoir opened at **Vyrnwy** by the Mayor - had a capacity of 4,500,000 gallons in connection with the Liverpool water scheme

Above: Tramcar No.268 is passing the baths in Speke Road, Garston - built in 1900 the tram was withdrawn in 1933

Above: These Liverpool policemen were photographed by the Police official photographer, GE Mills, Carbonora, in 1913

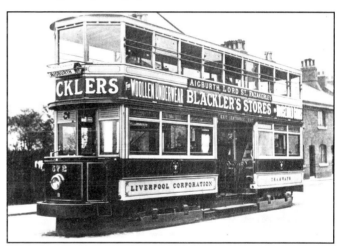

*Above:- Experimental Tramcar No. 572, was built in 1913. It is seen in **Fazakerley**. The design was not successful and after years of storage it was scrapped in 1929*

*Left: The **New Brighton** ferry boat on the left with passengers looking towards the landing stage, is behind the Woodside luggage boat which is seen carrying two big cars*

Left: The Royal Carriage carrying the King and Queen is seen entering the Liverpool Exhibition of 1913, followed by a mounted escort - either side is a parade of Boy Scouts

Below: The Fun Fair and 'Exhibition Express' at the Liverpool Exhibition

Above: Lord Derby saluting the King and Queen in front of St George's Hall on the occasion of their visit to open the new Gladstone Dock at **Seaforth** (see below)

Left: This topiary crown in **Sefton** Park was created for the Royal Visit

Below: HRH King George V and Queen Mary opened the new Mersey Docks & Harbour Board's Gladstone Dock at **Seaforth** that was described at the time as "the largest dock in the world" - the men seen in the bottom of the dock give an idea of its enormous size. There was a great pageant of ships in the River Mersey led by two cruisers HMS Liverpool *and* Lancaster

Jan 1   Old training ship *Indefatigable* replaced by HMS *Phaeton* and presented to the Liverpool Sea Training Homes

Feb 23 St Barnabas, **Mossley Hill** dedicated - cost £25,000

Mar 16 White Star Liner *Lusitania* established a new average speed record by steaming 618 knots in 24 hours at an average speed of 26.7 knots

Apr 21 Big fire at Huskisson Dock

Apr 29 Liverpool Merchants' Guild incorporated by Royal Charter

July 23 Countess of Derby opened the "Sir Alfred Jones" ward of the Liverpool School of Tropical Medicine at the Royal Infirmary

Aug 4   Great Britain declared war on Germany

Sept 7 Gladstone Dock Station opened on the Lancashire & Yorkshire Railway line[ISOLRS]

Oct 7   Canadian Pacific Railway Co's new twin screw steamer *Missionable* sailed on her maiden voyage from Liverpool to Quebec and Montreal

Nov 25 Wesleyan Church opened at **Warbreck Moor**

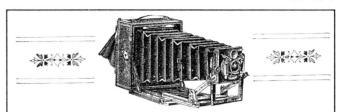

Right: St Nicholas' Church is seen on the left behind the girders of the Liverpool Overhead Railway - to the right are enclosed steps leading up either side to the LOR Pier Head Station. The Overhead Railway, which was 6.5 miles long, linked **Seaforth** at the north end and **Dingle** at the south end with a total of 17 stations

Left: Tramcar No.510, which was built at Lambeth Road in 1908, is seen progressing down Lord Street. This was one of the designated 'First Class' only trams. 'First Class' was abolished in 1923 but the car survived until 1937

1914

The crowds are gathered to welcome the King and Queen on their visit to Liverpool

- Nurses' Home opened for **Bootle** General Hospital in memory of King Edward VII - cost £6,000

Jan 16   Schooner *Kate* sank in the Mersey after a collision with the White Star tug *Magnetic* - three of the crew were lost

Feb 24   Liverpool ship *Western Coast* sunk by German submarine off Beachy Head [over 40 Liverpool based ships reported sunk by German submarines in 1915 according to *Kelly's Directory*]

Mar 9   Pleasure steamer *Princess Victoria* sunk by a German submarine about 18 miles from the Mersey

May   **Everton** FC 1st Division League Champions 1914/15 season

May 7   Cunard liner *Lusitania* sunk by a German submarine off the Old Head of Kinsale with a loss of over 1,300 lives including many women and children. Also most of the crew came from Merseyside - this led to the 'Lusitania Riots' (*see article*)

June 7   Centenary of the Liverpool Savings Bank

July 10   Day and Sunday Schools for the Parish of St Anne, **Stanley** opened

Aug 20   White Star liner *Arabic* sunk off the South coast of Ireland with the loss of 32 lives

Oct   Two ambulances were presented to the Red Cross by employees of the Cunard Line in memory of those lost on the *Lusitania*[RMSL] (*see photo*)

Dec 12   White Star liner *Britannic* arrived in the Mersey from Belfast - taken over by the Admiralty

Above: Some of the wounded soldiers from Ward Y of the Belmont Military Hospital are seen with their nursing staff

Above: Sefton Park was opened in 1870 - this six-arched sandstone bridge spanned the boating lake

Above: The Boat House is seen on the right at Newsham Park with an odd-looking structure on the left - possibly hectagonal - with a domed roof

Following the sinking of the Cunard Liner *Lusitania* by a German submarine on 7 May 1915, with most of the crew being from Merseyside, anti-German feeling was running high in Liverpool. Rioting began in Liverpool on Saturday evening 8 May. The police were helpless in controlling the angry crowds who firstly attacked German and Austrian named businesses in Liverpool. The shops, businesses or sometimes private homes were stoned, looted - with the contents being thrown onto the street and set on fire. The rioting continued the following day and by Monday had moved across the Mersey to Birkenhead where the same treatment was carried out. The damage caused by the rioters was both destructive and widespread with over 200 shops and houses in Liverpool alone wrecked or damaged at an estimated cost of £40,000 - £50,000[MM&MIB]

Five months after the sinking of the Lusitania *in May 1915, Directors, staff and crews of the Cunard Line raised funds in memory of those who died in the incident and purchased the* Lusitania *Ambulance (see below) as a memorial to those who lost their lives in the tragedy. Mrs AA Booth presented it to the British Red Cross Society in front of the Cunard Building (see above)*[RMSL]

Above: A branch of Boots the Chemist, at 110-112a Bold Street, is on the left, next
to Thomas Armstrong and Brother, the Optician with the spectacles sign outside

Above: The Lord Mayor of Liverpool is pictured on the steps of
St George's Hall 21 March 1915 to the right of Lord Kitchener
who was visiting Liverpool on a recruitment campaign and to
review the 12,000 locally recruited men who marched past St
George's Hall and along Lime Street

Above: This large house at 54 Ullet Road was taken over by
the Military and used as a hospital for the wounded - the
people of Liverpool could see and hear the harsh reality of war

Above: The crowds are lining Lime Street to see the 17th Battalion The King's (Liverpool Regiment) marching towards London
Road on 20 March 1915 - the day Lord Kitchener reviewed all the new troops who were training in the area (see above)

- Cunard National Shell factory at **Bootle** was the first factory in the country to manufacture shells using female labour

Jan   Cunard liner *Aquitania* converted to troopship at Gladstone Dock

May   *Olympic* converted to troopship at Gladstone Dock with 'dazzle' painting

June 18   Fire at *Imperial Hotel*, Lime Street, three people killed

Oct 29   Inauguration of the Jewish Centre, Princes Road

Dec 1   St James' Station closed on the Cheshire Lines Committee line[ISOLRS]

Above: Nurses at the Highfield Military Hospital in Liverpool where they saw the realities of the war at first hand

Above: Central Hall was erected in Renshaw Street, on the site of a Unitarian Chapel, in 1905 - costing over £50,000 it seated over 3,100 people

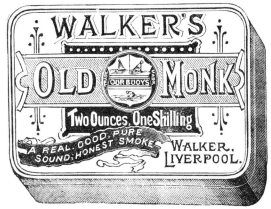
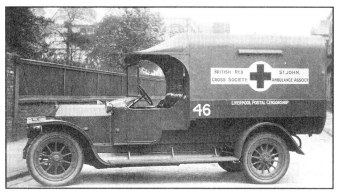

Above: This British Red Cross Society/St John's Ambulance Association ambulance No.46 was paid for by workers at the Liverpool Postal Censorship

Left: *This was a picture of the Cunard National Shell Factory at **Bootle** where the author's Grandfather, Alexander Galbraith, was General Manager - it was the first factory in the country to manufacture shells produced by lady operators*

1917

- **Woolton** Wood Park open to the public
- Feb *Celtic* mined off Mersey Bar - repairs at Gladstone Dock
- Mar 1 **Garston** Church Road Station closed on the London & North Western Railway line[ISOLRS]
- Apr 3 Unveiling of memorial to Sgt. David Jones, VC - a former pupil of Heyworth Street School
- Apr 15 **Garston** Dock Station closed on the London & North Western Railway line[ISOLRS]
- July 31 Commercial Reference Library opened in Exchange Buildings
- Aug 11 Death announced of Captain Noel Chavasse VC, son of the Bishop of Liverpool[LDPCE]
- Dec 28 No.1 Pilot Boat SS *Alfred H Read* sunk by enemy action off the Bar Lightship with the loss of life

Above: White Star liner Cretic *was requisitioned from May 1917 to February 1919 and used as a troop ship - seen here with American troops docked at Liverpool[WS]*

RING UP 1192 ROYAL FOR
Taxi-Cars and Private Touring Cars *Always Ready*
12 & 14, Norton St., London Rd., LIVERPOOL.
J. ANSONIA & CO., LTD.   TELEPHONE NO. 1192 ROYAL.

Above: Volunteer nurses sitting at tables, bandage rolling - for the Red Cross - the author's Grandmother, Eliza Boumphrey, is the middle lady of the three standing on the right

Above: This British tank was in fact a converted Liverpool tram which was used as an office where the public were encouraged to buy War Bonds - ironically the base of the tram was that of a German tram which was in service from 1898 to 1902

Right: Tram No.389, built by Dick Kerr in 1901 - originally open-topped it was covered in 1904 and is seen here, painted white as a First Class only car, in Church Street

Jan 1 **Walton-on-the-Hill** Station closed on the Cheshire Lines Committee line[ISOLRS]

Feb 5 Anchor liner *Tuscania* bringing over USA troops to Liverpool, was torpedoed off the Irish Coast with a loss of over 200 lives

Oct 18 Rt. Hon. John Hodge MP, Minister of Pensions, addressed a meeting at the Town Hall for the King's Fund

Oct 18 Bequest under the will of the late JH Welsford of the residue of his estate (estimated at £700,000) to be divided between The Liverpool Shipbrokers' Benevolent Society and the Cathedral Building Fund

Nov 11 Peace - First World War comes to an end - at the eleventh hour on the eleventh day of the eleventh month

Camp Life at PRESCOT --- I DON'T think !

Above: This First World War comic postcard was sent in 1918 from the Military Camp based at Prescot

Left: Review of the USA troops in front of St George's Hall on Independence Day 4 July 1918

Owen Owen, a twenty-year old Welshman, arrived in Liverpool in 1868, having worked in his uncle's drapery in Bath. He set up business renting 119-121, London Road. His policy was to keep his profit as low as possible and by undercutting his competitors, ensure a rapid turnover. Business boomed and within five years he employed 120 people and in 1876 purchased 119 - 123 London Road for £13,500, which became known as Audley House. By the turn of the century Owen Owen's store had become one of the biggest and most fascinating in the North, with over 400 employees - many being accommodated in the firm's own hostels, the male staff in Stafford Street and the female assistants in Shaw Street. Instead of spending his wealth on new stores, he invested in shares and property. After he died in 1910, there was no obvious leader, so business steadily declined and in the 1920s a new board was appointed. Under the new Chairman, Mr A Thomas, they moved to new premises in Clayton Square which was not an immediate success and in 1926 a new Chairman, Mr Duncan Norman, was appointed. The company's fortunes changed when Owen Owen merged with a smaller, successful business TJ Hughes with 'TJ's' moving their business into part of the vacant London Road store opening 7 October 1927. Business there was very successful with TJ's taking over the whole building. It continued to flourish but in 1932, due to being convinced he had an incurable illness, TJ Hughes sold the business to Owen Owen Ltd but died two years later in tragic circumstances. Duncan Norman, who had married Owen Owen's daughter, Dilys in 1918, brought in younger people from within the company to the board and with fresh ideas,

Everything for Ladies' and Children's Wear.

One of the largest Drapery and Furnishing Stores in the Kingdom.

OWEN OWEN LD., London Road, Liverpool.

the company flourished. Owen Owen's new policy of going upmarket changed and followed the more successful business methods of TJ's and the emphasis changed to lower prices and rapid turnover. Helped by improved buying methods and advertising techniques, trade expanded rapidly and in 1935 suitable new sites were sought - the first one being Coventry which opened in 1937 followed by Preston. During the war, the Liverpool stores survived major damage but Coventry was destroyed - luckily with no fatalities. After the War other stores were opened and by 1957 Owen Owen stores were in Liverpool, Preston Coventry, Southampton, Doncaster and TJ's in Liverpool and Blackpool as well as a store in Canada.[OO]

1919

Feb 28   Queen Victoria Nursing Association's new Nursing Home opened at **Bootle** by Sir Thomas Royden

Mar 1   **Garston** Church Road Station re-opened on the London & North Western Railway line[ISOLRS]

Mar 27   Admiral Sir David Beatty arrived in the Mersey aboard HMS *Queen Elizabeth*

Mar 31   Collapse of seven storey warehouse in Back Goree with loss of life - later rebuilt and called The Strand

May 5   **Garston** Dock Station re-opened on the London & North Western Railway line[ISOLRS]

July 24   Nurse Alice Jones was murdered on the steps of the Northern Hospital, Liverpool, when Joseph Hutty, an American soldier shot her dead. He had been fighting for the Canadians in France and was being treated in the hospital for severe 'shell shock'. Although originally sentenced to death, he was eventually reprieved[LNH]

July 30   National Police Strike - more policemen on strike in Liverpool than anywhere else in the country[LPS] (*see article and photos next page*)

Nov   First Corporation homes built at **Bootle** - 310 non-parlour and parlour houses built - they had large gardens and trees were planted along the roads

Above: This comic postcard shows a boy on the left catching a glimpse of a lady holding up her skirt and showing her stockings! - quite risque for 1919!

Below: This panoramic view of the River Mersey taken from the Royal Liver Building, shows how busy the river and port were just after the First World War - with over 60 ships from liners to ferry boats and fishing vessels

The Liverpool Police Strike of 1919 was triggered off when on Thursday 30 July a strike was called by the trade union representing the policemen of this country. The National Union of Police and Prison officers had been formed in 1913 and increased membership significantly with the Liverpool branch having 99% membership by 1919. A committee under Lord Desborough recommended that the police should be represented by a federation, confined to Police Officers. Following this, the Government brought in the 1919 Police Act which stated that a policeman could not belong to a trade union. At this time many policemen considered their pay and conditions to be worse than that of a general labourer who could expect a minimum of £3. 7 shillings per week whereas a policeman's minimum was £2. 3 shillings per week with a war bonus of 12 shillings and then 2/6d per child allowance and an annual increase of 1/- to a maximum of £4. 3 shillings after 21 years service. On top of this they only had one day off every 14 days worked and would expect to work longer than their 8 hours per day for no extra pay - with Constables working an average of 78 hours per week.

The Desborough Committee agreed that most of their complaints should be met but that the Police Union be replaced by a Police Federation which could not deal with discipline or promotion complaints and it was made unlawful to join the Police Union. The strike was called to protest against this.

The strike became effective from 10pm on Thursday 30 July. By the following day 632 policemen were on strike in Liverpool and although policemen in London had been instantly dismissed, the Liverpool strikers were given the chance to return by 8pm on Friday 1 August. At that time a meeting of strikers was held at St George's Plateau with about 600 policemen attending. In all 929 Policemen from Liverpool and 50 from Bootle went on strike out of 2271 and 75 respectively.

Special Constables were called up and advertisements were placed in local papers to replace the vacancies left by the sacked strikers. The Lord Mayor placed a newspaper advert on 1 August asking for volunteers to assist in the maintenance of Law and Order in the City. The following day six lorries with troops arrived and were accommodated in St George's Hall. Four tanks also arrived and by Monday a further 2,500 troops and four tanks arrived plus the battleship *Valiant* with two destroyers - one to protect the port and docks - the other went to **Birkenhead.**

Rioting began on Friday evening 1 August with mainly young men taking advantage of the lack of policemen. The situation became worse after midnight when shops in Byrom Street, Great Homer Street and Scotland Road (*see photo*) were broken into and looted - they went for Pawnbrokers and Jewellers initially then shoe and clothes shops - in all about 20 shops were attacked.

On Saturday 2 August the Riot Act was read in Scotland Road, soldiers fired above the heads of rioters and police made repeated baton charges. By Sunday night the police had enrolled 600 Special Constables and recalled 250 war-time Special Constables to deal with the violence and protect banks and businesses. By Monday night further volunteers were recruited which helped to keep the incidents to a minimum. The troops stayed until the end of the month with the City Council being left with a bill of £122,000 for riot damage plus the cost of the army.

Due to the lack of support from other unions and the Police Union running out of funds, the strike was over and policing of the city had almost returned to normal by the middle of the month. None of the policemen who had gone on strike were reinstated but those who stayed on duty received special grants from the Watch Committee for their loyalty[LPS]

Left: During the National Police Strike there were more policemen on strike in Liverpool than anywhere else in the country. This view of Scotland Road during the riots shows that people were not afraid to go onto the streets, the windows of many shops are boarded up and there are several policemen mingling with the crowds[LPS]

Right: Workmen are boarding up 33 London Road, the shop of Joseph Ball & Son, Jewellers; No.35 Van Ralty's photographer's shop and 37-43 Beaty Bros, High Class Tailors also had boarding erected. Ironically the building next to Balls was a pub The Clock which is probably where some of the looters drank before committing their crimes. The looters took advantage of the lack of police as just under 1,000 were on strike in Liverpool. However, the remaining 1,300 were joined by newly recruited Specials and also over 2,500 soldiers. The looters would break into the shop and toss out goods to those waiting in the street. Initially the troops would advance on the looters with fixed bayonets followed some way behind by police and Specials with truncheons[TNTPWOS]

1920

Apr 10   An outbreak of fire at a six-floor cotton warehouse in Errington Street, the property of Messrs. JH Burns, causes damage estimated at £50,000

May   *Acquitania* and *Olympic* had their hulls repainted at Gladstone Dock

July 8   Mr WH Gilmour appointed to the Chair of Dental Surgery at Liverpool University, endowed by Alderman LS Cohen with a gift of £5,000 - this being the first Chair in Dentistry established in an English University

Aug 5   Collision of two trams at the bottom of James Street, caused injuries to seven people

Aug 30   Due to a printers' strike, the *Liverpool Courier* failed to appear for the first time for 112 years - strike ended September 18

Sept 1   Strike of Shipwrights in the Mersey District - lasted 10 weeks

Oct 4   Mr CJ Williamson offered his residence and estate, Camp Hill, **Woolton**, to the Liverpool Corporation for use by the public

Oct 24   Discovery of a Sinn Fein plot for blowing up the Dock Gates at Liverpool - captured documents read out in the House of Commons by Sir Hamar Greenwood

Dec 3   Violent gale prevents all sailings from the Mersey

Above: Built at Lambeth Road tramway works by men accustomed to building trams. It was top heavy so its roof and upper deck windows were removed and it ran as an open topper

Above: The Cunard liner *Acquitania is pictured in Gladstone Dock - she had a post-war refit at Hunter's Tyneside yard and here at Gladstone Dock - she was the first merchant ship to be fitted with a Gyro Compass after the First World War*

*Above: This Liverpool Corporation Bellamy 62 seater tram was photographed in West Derby Road, **Tuebrook** - it came into service in 1911, finishing in 1938*

DELIGHTFUL SEA TRIPS
FROM
LIVERPOOL to NORTH WALES.

Every Day by the " LA MARGUERITE " at 10-45 a.m.
For LLANDUDNO, BEAUMARIS, BANGOR, and MENAI BRIDGE, due back
7-30 p.m., allowing 4 hours ashore at Llandudno.
EXTRA SAILINGS AT WEEK-ENDS FROM LIVERPOOL.

Daily Coast Excursions, at Low Fares, from LLANDUDNO and STRAITS
To CARNARVON, HOLYHEAD, DOUGLAS, BLACKPOOL, and other places by
Steamers "ST. TUDNO," "ST. ELVIES," and "SNOWDON."

Contracts, available for all Sailings, Weekly, 12/6; Fortnightly, 20/-;
Monthly, 27/6.
Apply The Liverpool and North Wales Steamship Co., Ltd., 40 Chapel St., Liverpool.
Telephone 6366.

Above: A range of transport is used by the traders at St John's Wholesale Vegetable Market from hand cart, horse and cart to wagon - the market was established here in 1866

Right: 1920 was the Centenary of George Hadfield's Liverpool Bone and Fertiliser Works - Hadfields was established in 1820 by Thomas Hadfield - they produced many different advertising postcards with a photograph of a local farmer who had won prizes for their turnips using Hadfield's Special Turnip Manure - the company was purchased by Fisons in 1935

1921

- Henry Tate & Sons Ltd amalgamated with Abraham Lyle & Sons Ltd - sugar production at their Love Lane refinery now 17,000 tons per week[LDPCE]

Mar 17　King George V and Queen Mary visit Liverpool for five days - during their stay they inspected the Ministry of Labour Local Training Centre, Rumney Road, **Kirkdale**; the Seamen's Orphanage; the Lord Roberts Memorial Workshops, Fontenoy Street; made presentation of books at St George's Hall to 200 children who lost their fathers during the Great War; attended the Spring Meeting at **Aintree** including the Grand National and attended a service at the Lady Chapel of Liverpool Cathedral

Census:　Population of Liverpool and suburbs 803,118 (an increase of 49,765 since 1911)

June　Dedication of the **West Derby** War Memorial (*see photo*)

June 29　Completion of new trunk telephone cable between Liverpool and **Chester**

July 5　HRH Prince of Wales pays a four-day visit to the area including: **Liverpool, Southport** and **Bootle**

Aug 15　**Formby** Lightship *Planet* sunk in collision with the steamer *Green Briar*

Sept 13　Unemployed and police in conflict in Liverpool - attempt to storm the Walker Art Gallery resulted in baton charge on raiders with 100 arrested and many injured[LDPCE]

Oct 22　The Earl of Derby unveiled the Cunard Steamship Company's War Memorial Column and **Rainhill** War memorial

Above: **Waterloo** *War Memorial erected in 1921*

Left: **West Derby** *War Memorial dedication June 1921*

Below: The sender of this postcard wrote that "I went to see this boat today" 23 April 1921 - a visit to Liverpool by one of the Royal Navy's warships

Apr 28   War Memorial unveiled in the Liverpool offices of the Canadian Pacific Railway by Col Campbell VC

May   Liverpool FC 1st Division League Champions for the 1921/22 season

May 15   War Memorial to the employees of W&R Jacob & Co unveiled at the **Aintree** Biscuit Factory

June 1   Fire at farm house in Wheaton Lane in **Huyton** destroyed several outhouses and a granary

June 10   Elder Dempster Recreation and Athletic Club opened at Oaklands Park, Barkhill Road **Aigburth**

July 23   Bishop of Liverpool unveiled the War Memorial at **Prescot** to the men from the **West Derby** Hundred who died in the Great War

Aug 21   Snapping of gangway at West Harrington Dock causes 25 men to be thrown into the water - six sustained severe injuries

Oct 2   Demolition completed of St Peter's Church

Oct 23   Irish Steamship *The Maigue* sinks in Wellington Dock

Nov 11   Unveiling of Cenotaph in front of St George's Hall erected as a memorial to the Liverpool men who fought and died in the Great War 1914-18

Nov 24   New Barclay's Bank building opened on corner of Rumford Street and Water Street

Dec 1   The Cabinet planned to provide work including the East Lancs Road from Liverpool to Manchester - to employ 20,000 men[LDPCE]

Dec 4   Princess Helena Victoria visited Liverpool in connection with Red Triangle Lads Club

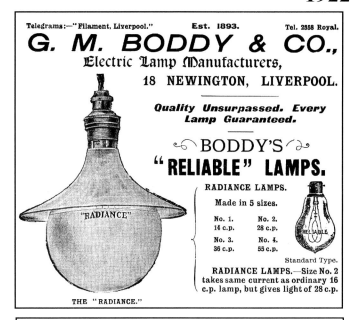

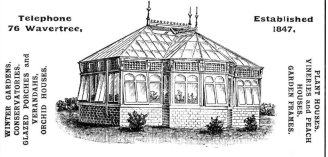

Above: This motley bunch of Liverpool University students are posing during the 1922 Rag Week

Below: The liner Majestic, belonging to Liverpool based White Star, was originally launched in 1914 for the Hamburg American line as the Bismark - she lay incomplete during the First World War and handed over in 1919 as prize - she was completed in 1922, the same year as her maiden voyage - sold for scrap in 1936 but not finally scrapped until 1943[WS]

1923

Feb 15   Steam Flat sunk off **Garston** - the crew of three were missing

Apr 10   Three boot shops in Tunnel Road burnt out

May   Liverpool FC 1st Division Champions for the 1922/23 season

May 14   Memorial unveiled in Ford Roman Catholic Cemetery to the first Roman Catholic Archbishop of Liverpool, Dr Thomas Whiteside

July 14   White Star Line building in James Street destroyed by fire caused by lightening

August   **Waterloo** & **Crosby** Motor Services start operations[LTVol2]

Oct 29   First Marconi Telegraph Office established in the provinces opened at 22 Chapel Street

Dec 16   The Union Steamship Co of New Zealand liner *Armagh* wrecked and sunk off **Hightown** - no loss of life

Left: Liverpool Corporation Tram No.141 is pictured in Lord Street - built by Dick Kerr in 1900, this 50 seater was withdrawn from service in 1923

Above: Liverpool Corporation Tramcar No.100 is pictured on route No.12 at the terminus in **West Derby** *Village*

Above: These 18th century buildings in Clayton Square were originally exclusive residential properties which were later converted into shops and offices

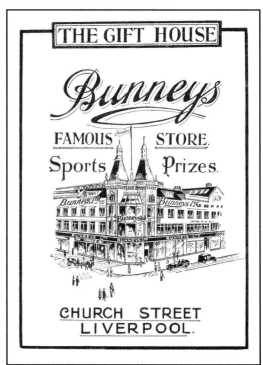
Above: This advertisement was for Bunneys store which was situated on the corner of Church Street and Whitechapel

Jan 21   Railway strike began[LDPCE]

Jan   Railway strike over - men return to work[LDPCE]

Feb 18   The old *Liverpool Empire Theatre* closed prior to demolition and being re-built[LDPCE]

Apr 30   New air services opened between Liverpool and Belfast operating once a day and taking over two hours

June 15   Start of a nine day visit of 23 warships to Liverpool - seen by over 262,000 people

July 14   All-night tramcar service began on certain routes for night workers and men from ships arriving overnight - double fares were charged

July 7   Gladstone Dock Station closed on the former Lancashire & Yorkshire Railway line[ISOLRS]

July 19   King George V and Queen Mary attended the consecration of Liverpool Cathedral

July 20   King George V and Queen Mary attended the dedication at Liverpool Cathedral of the North transept as a War Memorial to the soldiers and sailors of Liverpool and district who fell in the Great War (*see photo*)

July 27   Collision at Lime Street Station between a crowded excursion train from London and a stationary engine - 16 people injured - luckily no serious damage caused

July 27   Home for orphan children given by the Liverpool Churches and opened as a memorial to the men of those churches who fell in the Great War 1914-18

Sept 3   Oil Jetty at **Dingle** Point damaged by steamer

Sept 28   Liverpool Memorial Hall opened by the Lord Mayor at Givenchy, France - in memory of the men of the 55th Division (West Lancs) who fought and fell there

Sept 30   The Government's offer of over £2.3 million towards the cost of the Mersey Tunnel was not acceptable[LDPCE]

Above: The crowd are seen cheering as King George V and Queen Mary are heading their procession following the dedication at Liverpool Cathedral of the North transept as a War Memorial to the soldiers and sailors of Liverpool and district who fell in the Great War

Above: There are six trams queueing up in Water Street behind two motor cars with two wagons on the right - one horse-drawn and the other motor

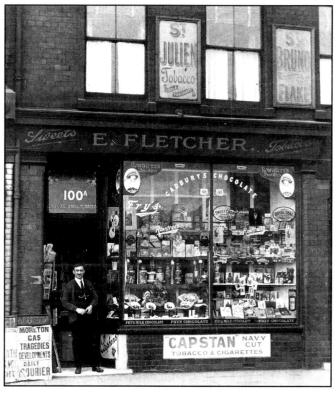

Above: Fletcher Sweets & Tobacco Shop at 100a Picton Road, Wavertree was typical of the small local shop which sold newspapers and there is even a teddy bear for sale

1925

- Thoroughgood's Breweries Ltd **Waterloo** was taken over by Threllfalls Brewery Co Ltd[WHATBG]
- **Seaforth** Sands 1st Station closed and passengers used the 2nd Station on the Liverpool Overhead Railway[ISOLRS]

Jan 17   Dedication of a memorial in the South Transept of Liverpool Cathedral in memory of the men of the 55th Division (West Lancs) who fell in the Great War

Feb 9   Princess Marie Louise visited the city to fulfil engagements with the Red Triangle Club - met by the Lord Mayor, they drove to the Cathedral and afterwards to the Town Hall for a Civic Reception and in the evening a Ball was held at the Adelphi Hotel

Feb 27   Liverpool City School of commerce opened by the Rt. Hon. Lord Eustace Percy MP, President of the Board of Education

Apr 14   The oil steamer *Invergoil*, owned by the British Mexican petroleum Co Ltd crashed into the **Dingle** Jetty and damaged 100ft. of staging

May 4   Juvenile Court in Crosshall - first in the country to be purpose built

Oct 3   Foundation stone laid for St Mark's Church, Edge Lane by A Hunter Crawford Esq

Oct 5   Liverpool Civic Week commenced - finished 10 October

Nov 3   Collision between two tramcars in Leece Street - 23 injured

Nov 14   The steamer *Cherry Branch* of the Nautilus Steamship Company caught fire in the Brocklebank Dock

Dec 16   Princess Mary, Viscountess Lascelles, inaugurated the first shaft to be sunk for the Mersey Tunnel (*see plans of tunnel*)

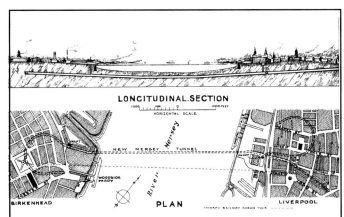

These cross sectional views of the Mersey Tunnel were printed in a souvenir programme to commemorate the ceremonial inauguration by her Royal Highness Princess Mary 16 December 1925

Above: This longitudinal section shows the plan of the tunnel below the River Mersey from Birkenhead on the left to Liverpool on the right - together with a map

Below: *This cross section of the proposed tunnel shows that the two centre lanes had motor vehicles and the two inside lanes horse-drawn vehicles, whilst pedestrians are seen walking through on either side! The cross-section also shows that only the top half was used for traffic - however, it was later proposed to run a tram system down the middle of the bottom section but was opposed by Mersey Ferries and Mersey Railway, and never got off the drawing board*

Above: Cripps, Sons & Co were described as: "Manufacturing Furriers, also high-class mantle, costume, millinery, blouses & underclothing, gloves and hosiery"

Jan 1   **Allerton** Hall and estate presented to Liverpool by the sons of Thomas Clarke in memory of their parents

July 26 Extension of Electric Power Station at Lister Drive

Aug 16   An earthquake which shook England was felt in Liverpool[LDPCE]

Oct 4   Work started on the new housing scheme in **Dingle**

Oct 18   Organ of Liverpool Cathedral dedicated

Oct 22   The British Enka Artificial Silk Factory opened

Above: Taken shortly after the replacemennt of Liverpool Overhead Railway Tramways by Waterloo & Crosby Motor Services - this ex London General bus TD5294 en route to **Seaforth** *Sands, is passing the junction with St Johns Road*

IN LIVERPOOL

And the Great Industrial and Commercial Areas encircling the City

PEOPLE READ THE

POST *Every Morning*

And at Night THE ECHO

NEWSPAPERS OF CHARACTER ENTERPRISE DEPENDABILITY & SOLID WORTH

Above: An advert for the Liverpool Post and Echo (see 1928)

Above: This postcard was sent in 1926 with the message "thought you might be interested in this picture, it is one of our new buses" - taken in Crosby Road Waterloo

Above: This illuminated Tramcar was decorated for the 1926 Liverpool Civic Week

JONATHAN EDMONDSON & CO LTD

WHOLESALE & EXPORT CONFECTIONERS

CHOCOLATE & TOFFEE MANUFACTURERS

FOX STREET LIVERPOOL

PURITY BRAND WORKS, FOX ST.   TOXTETH WORKS, WAVERTREE

*Telephones: North. 863/4
Wavertree. 44
Wires: Celebrated*

Left: The nearest of the trams in Dale Street is No.119, built at Lambeth Road in 1923 and withdrawn in 1948 - J Lyons & Co Popular State Cafe is pictured on the right

1926

Above: This glacial 'erratic' boulder consisting of Gypsum, estimated at 25 tons, is seen in Liverpool Road, **Crosby**. It was found in 1898 embedded in boulder clay at a depth of 20 feet below the surface in a field in Cooks Lane, **Great Crosby**. Mr Edward Peters presented it to the District Council who located it here in 1901. It was removed in 1926 to its present site in Coronation Park - a branch of John Irwin's grocery shops is seen in the background (at time of printing this publication this shop was Pritchard's bookshop, but about to be demolished - see also 1950 for Irwin's history)[BOCOG]

Right: A comic postcard of **Bootle** with a catch-phrase of the time

ONE OF THE D-HUCKS.
At BOOTLE.

The Liverpool Co-operative Society advertised their assets in the Liverpool Civic Week Official Programme and Handbook *October 1926 which included:- 2 Grocery Stores, 15 Butchery Stores, 31 Bread Shops, 12 Drapery, 13 Boots, 4 Tailoring and 3 Furnishing Departments; a Central Dairy and 37 Branch Dairies, Bread and Confectionery Bakeries, a Boot Repairing Factory, Coal Depots, a Works Department and a Dairy Farm*

Mar 8	To make room for the Cenotaph, the statue of Lord Beaconsfield was removed from the plateau of St George's Hall to a new position on the steps
Mar 19	A long-distance motor-coach service between Liverpool and Glasgow started
Apr 14	**Clubmoor** Station opened on Cheshire Lines Committee railway[ISOLRS]
Apr 30	Greyhound Racing using electronic hares first introduced into Liverpool
May 13	Liverpool University Memorial to all those who fell in the Great War unveiled by Lord Derby
May 30	Marsh Lane Baths in **Bootle** re-opened - having been converted to a covered-in bath (*see 1902*)[BOH]
July 9	Liverpool College for Girls **Huyton** dedicated by the Bishop of Liverpool
July 18	King of Egypt visited Liverpool
July 19	HRH King George V and Queen Mary opened Gladstone Docks - cost £7,500,000 - largest dock in the world (*see photos and article*)
Aug 13	HMS *Rodney* built at Cammell Laird left the Mersey for Portsmouth
Sept 22	First wedding at Liverpool Cathedral solemnised
Sept 24	Liverpool Civic Week and Air Pageant started
Oct 6	**Knotty Ash** Estate bought by the Corporation for housing
Oct 7	TJ Hughes moved into their new London Road store
Oct 24	Archbishop of Liverpool laid the foundation stone of the Roman Catholic Church of Christ the King
Nov 10	Miss Margaret Bevan was elected Lord Mayor of Liverpool[LDPCE]
Nov 21	King Feisal of Iraq visited Liverpool
Dec 5	Gladstone Graving Dock opened to shipping
Dec 10	Liverpool Press Club premises opened in St George's Buildings, Lime Street

HM Queen Mary with The Lord Mayor of Liverpool Clr Fredk. C Bowring with his wife, on the occasion of the Royal visit to Liverpool when King George V and Queen Mary opened Gladstone Docks - cost £7,500,000 and was then the largest dock in the world (see below)

*King George V and Queen Mary visited Liverpool on 19 July 1927 to open the new Gladstone Dock (see photo). They arrived at Riverside Station then proceeded to the Town Hall where they were welcomed by the Lord Mayor; on to the Town Hall for lunch then to the Landing Stage where they boarded the SS Galatea and proceeded to open Gladstone Dock. They eventually left for London via **Bootle** (Oriel) Station.*

***The Gladstone Dock Estate**, which cost £7,500,000 was one of the largest dock complexes in the world at that time. The great lock into the Mersey was 1,070 ft. long and 130 ft. wide. The depth on the sills at normal high tide was about 50 ft. and at low tide 22ft. - which meant that it could accommodate the largest ships in the world at half-tide[LatMVol1]*

Above: *The scale of the almost completed new Gladstone Dock system can be judged by the size of the railway wagons in the foreground and the men facing the photographer near the left corner of the three-storied concrete transit sheds - see details of the dock system above*

Left: This postcard, sent in 1927, shows St John's Gardens and the rear of St George's Hall - the foreground was later to be the entrance/exit to the Mersey Tunnel (see 1934)

CIVIC WEEK.

MARATHON RACE ROUND LIVERPOOL

ON

Wednesday, September 28th

Course of 26 miles.

Start from St. George's Hall, 3-30 p.m.

See the finish at Liverpool F C. Ground, Anfield (available by kind permission of the directors).

Match between Boys of Liverpool and Boys of Bootle while you wait.

International Runners will compete.

*Above: St Johns Road **Waterloo** with the Westminster Bank Limited on the corner*

*Above: Three Guy double-decker buses described as "The New Wonder" Municipal motor omnibuses and "The Old Times" original Liverpool-Chester and Shrewsbury Stage Coach (on the left) in front of Allerton House, **Allerton** - one of the stopping points for the 'Tour Around Liverpool' during the Liverpool Civic Week 24 September to 1 October 1927*

Above: This triple-screw White Star liner Laurentic (II) was launched 16 June 1927 - her maiden voyage from Liverpool to New York was on 12 November 1927. She collided with the steamer Lurigethan October 1932 - taken over by Cunard White Star in 1934 - collided again, this time with with Blue Star Liner Napier Star in the Irish Sea - laid up at Millbrook, Southampton - September 1936 sailed from Southampton with troops for Palestine - laid up on return - took part in Merchant Week at Millbrook July 1937 - converted in 1939 to an armed merchant cruiser - she was torpedoed and sunk on 3 November 1940 off Bloody Foreland by U-boat U.99

- Rushworth & Draper celebrated their centenary - still under family control[LDPCE]

Mar 6 HRH Prince Henry (Duke of Gloucester) visited Liverpool to launch the British Empire Cancer Fund

Apr 3 Ceremony of 'breaking through' the Mersey Tunnel was performed when the final section of rock was breached (*see photo*)

May **Everton** FC 1st Division Champions 1927/28 (*see Dixie Dean on next page*)

June 16 Peter Pan Statue unveiled in **Sefton** Park and was celebrated by a pageant (*see photo*)

July 3 First meeting of the Liverpool and District Aero Club

Aug 14 First overnight motor coach service in Europe to provide sleeping bunks started from Liverpool to London

Sept 24 Fred Astaire and his wife, Adele, appeared at the *Liverpool Empire* in 'Funny Face' (*see programme below*)

Sept 24 Experimental Air Line Service between Liverpool and Belfast inaugurated

Oct 17 The Liverpool Corporation's new Edge Lane tram and bus building and repair works opened on a 15.5 acre site - cost £385,000 - this was originally the site for the 1887 Jubilee Exhibition and later the Tournament Hall

Oct 24 An agreement had been reached between Lord Sefton and Sefton RDC confirming that **Aintree** Racecourse would be available for the next 50 years to host the Grand National - after that period it would continue as an open space and could be used for sport[LDPCE]

Above: On 3 April 1927 the momentous occasion took place when the Lord Mayor of Liverpool, Miss Margaret Bevan, and the Mayor of Birkenhead, Alderman F Naylor, shook hands at the point where the tunneling from each side of the Queeensway Mersey Tunnel met in the middle. They were transported from their respective entrances to the dividing wall in toast-rack carriages and accommodated on wooden platforms raised half-way to the roof. Sir Archibald Salvidge, the Chairman of the Mersey Tunnel Joint Committee, made the breakthrough - they can be seen wearing oilskins, sou'-westers and gum boots, due to the wet and dirty conditions underground[TSOTMTQ]

LIVERPOOL EMPIRE
PROPRIETORS: MOSS' EMPIRES LTD.
Managing Director - R. H. GILLESPIE   Manager and Licensee - GEO. MANNERS
Musical Director - ALBERT MOORE

MONDAYS, SEPT. 24th and OCT. 1st

Nightly at 7-30. For Two Weeks
MATINEES each WEDNESDAY and SATURDAY at 2-30

ALFRED BUTT and LEE EPHRAIM
WITH
ALEX. A. AARONS and VINTON FREEDLEY
PRESENT

FRED ASTAIRE   ADELE ASTAIRE
AND
LESLIE HENSON
IN
A NEW MUSICAL COMEDY

"FUNNY FACE"

Music by GEORGE GERSHWIN
Book by FRED THOMPSON and PAUL GERARD SMITH. Lyrics by IRA GERSHWIN.
Dances and Ensembles created by ROBERT CONNOLLY and Staged by ELSIE NEAL.

THE PLAY PRODUCED BY FELIX EDWARDES

Above: Fred Astaire and his wife Adele appeared at the Liverpool Empire in 'Funny Face' for two weeks from 24th September

Left: *This Peter Pan Statue was made by Sir George Frampton and donated to* **Sefton** *Park by a local businessman, George Audley, who saw the original in Kensington Gardens, London and persuaded Frampton to cast a replica for the children of Liverpool - it is one of only four ever cast, the other two being in Australia and Canada. It was sited close to the cafe and aviary, being unveiled by a relative of JM Barrie, the author of Peter Pan, on 16 June 1928*

Above: *Liverpool Football Club playing staff and officials for the 1928/29 season*
[photographer GE Mills, Carbonora]

Right: *Dixie Dean, signed by Everton FC in*
1925 from Tranmere Rovers FC for £3,000
scored 60 goals in a season for Everton - a
record that has never been beaten

Above: *This* Liverpool Post & Echo *branch is advertising a*
£200 prize to be won in the Weekly Post *- filling almost every*
available space on the front of the building! The Liverpool
Daily Post *was founded in 1855 and in 1879, the* Liverpool
Echo *was launched*

- Eleanor Rathbone, a leading Women's Suffrage campaigner became Liverpool's first woman MP
Apr 29   Liverpool section of the East Lancashire Road was opened by the Lord Mayor
Aug 1   **Warbreck** Station opened on the Cheshire Lines Committee line[ISOLRS]
Aug 5   Royal National Welsh Eisteddfod opened in **Sefton** Park by the Lord Mayor
Sept 18   Dove Park, **Woolton** with 17 acres grounds, present to the Liverpool Corporation for the use of the public
Oct 15   French steamer *Oklahoma* destroyed by fire in Sandon Dock
Nov 30   St Andrew's Church, **Clubmoor**, consecrated by the Bishop of Liverpool
Dec   Liverpool & District Ramblers Federation founded the Merseyside Youth Hostels Association - the first organised group in the country to establish Youth Hostels

Above: This Liverpool Corporation bus KD 6499 was one of nine Thornycroft single-decker buses which came into service in 1929 - they had all been taken out of service by 1937 - it is pictured in Islington

Above: The Adelphi Hotel *in Ranelagh Place was opened in 1912, designed by Frank Atkinson, who also designed Selfridges in Oxford Street, London, it was originally intended to enclose a courtyard but the back was never built - Brownlow Hill is off to the right*

A reference book of schools for parents dated 1929 describes **Holmwood Preparatory School** at **Formby** as follows:- Holmwood is a Preparatory School preparing about 100 boys (aged 7 - 14) for the Public Schools and Dartmouth. The school stands in its own grounds of about 10 acres and is in open country about 1.5 miles from the Lancashire coast. There is a School Chapel with resident Chaplain; Gymnasium; two Pavilions and a Sanitorium. Activities include: Cricket; Football; Shooting; Boxing; Swimming; Physical Drill; Riding; Acting; Music and Dancing. There is a Preparatory School (Netherby) for boys from five until they are ready to pass into Holmwood [The school site was developed for housing in the late 1990s with the Holm Wood leased to the Woodland Trust for 125 years on a pepper-corn rent]

Below: This postcard of 'The Pirate Ship' in **Sefton** *Park, Liverpool, was posted in 1929 - at the time there was a 'Wendy House' and statue of Peter Pan close by (see 1928). It is said that this was converted from a lifeboat by the apprentices of Cammell Laird Shipyard,* **Birkenhead**

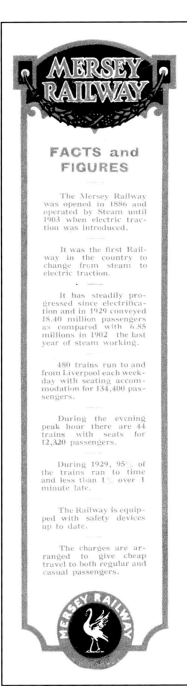

MERSEY RAILWAY

FACTS and FIGURES

The Mersey Railway was opened in 1886 and operated by Steam until 1903 when electric traction was introduced.

It was the first Railway in the country to change from steam to electric traction.

It has steadily progressed since electrification and in 1929 conveyed 18.40 million passengers as compared with 6.85 millions in 1902 the last year of steam working.

480 trains run to and from Liverpool each weekday with seating accommodation for 134,400 passengers.

During the evening peak hour there are 44 trains with seats for 12,320 passengers.

During 1929, 95% of the trains ran to time and less than 1% over 1 minute late.

The Railway is equipped with safety devices up to date.

The charges are arranged to give cheap travel to both regular and casual passengers.

Left: Both sides of a Mersey Railway bookmark printed about 1930 which gave 'Facts and Figures' about the railway

Below: The White Star liner Britannic *(III) was launched 6 August 1929 and her maiden voyage from Liverpool to New York was via Belfast and Glasgow on 28 June 1930. She was the largest motor ship in the world having survived the whole of the Second World War, she returned and was refitted in 1947 - scrapped in 1960*[WS]

May 31 Warrington Church of England Training College opened

June 5 Liverpool Council approved to sell the Brownlow Hill site to the Roman Catholics to build a Cathedral[LDPCE]

June 11 Brownlow Hill Workhouse site sold by the Liverpool City Council for the Roman Catholic Cathedral site

June 16 Gladstone Dock Station opened on the Liverpool Overhead Railway[ISOLRS]

Sept 10 The first official party walked through the Mersey Tunnel[LDPCE]

Sept 22 **Speke** Station closed on the LMS Railway[ISOLRS]

Oct 13 Centenary of the opening of the Liverpool and Manchester Railway - celebrated with a Pageant of Transport (*see photos*)

Oct 29 Road subsidence in Dale Street followed by explosions and fire - damage estimated at £50,000

Nov 11 Cenotaph in memory of those from Liverpool who fell in the Great War unveiled by the Earl of Derby

These two postcards were published to celebrate the Centenary of the first railway from Liverpool to Manchester in 1830:-

Above: Part of the 1930 Railway Pageant where a stagecoach has been just held up by highwaymen
Below: LMS Railway, Liverpool September 1930 and the 'Lion' & replica coaches, Liverpool & Manchester Railway 1830

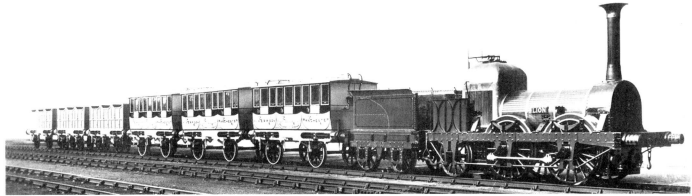

Above: *The paddle steamer* St Elvies *leaving Liverpool on her last trip to North Wales. Launched in 1896, she was a Minesweeper during the First World War and was broken up on the Wirral side of the Mersey at **New Ferry** in 1930*

Above: A 1930s scene in Church Street Liverpool with the Compton Hotel *behind and to the left of the tram, the sign on the right advertises 'Geranium Day' for the Liverpool Hospital Board*

Above: A comic postcard with a circular view of the Queen Victoria Monument and the caption "Looking Round Liverpool" - sent 1930

Above: This publicity postcard was for Macshane's Motors Ltd who ran a bus service from Liverpool to London via Chester, Birmingham, Stratford and Oxford and whose Liverpool office was at 5 Commutation Row. In 1931 the Traffic Commissioners handed out licences for the **Bootle** Bus Service to Macshanes ahead of Ribble. Following protests from Ribble and the Liverpool Corporation, which went as high as the Ministry of Transport and the House of Commons - the licences were revoked and handed to Ribble in 1933

Above: Pier Head Station is pictured on the immediate left on the Liverpool Overhead Railway, which disappears into the distance - St Nicholas' Church is on the right beyond the Hall Line offices

Jan 1   **Childwall** Station closed on Cheshire Lines Railway[ISOLRS]

Apr 21   Cinemas to be legalised for Sunday opening[LDPCE]

June 20   Brotherton Park, the gift of Lord Brotherton, opened

July 30   The Royal Lancashire Show opened - lasted four days

Aug 29   Start of the Liverpool Shipping Week was celebrated with a Nautical Pageant and an Exhibition held in St George's Hall

Sept 14   The abattoir and live cattle market opened - built by Liverpool Corporation at Stanley - cost £670,000 - opened by the Earl of Derby

Oct 4   The Very Reverend FW Dwelly was installed as the first Dean of Liverpool

Oct 30   Mapleton's Nut factory was destroyed by fire - over 200 people out of work

Nov 23   The Earl of Derby laid the foundation stone of the Radium Institute and Hospital for Cancer and Skin Diseases

Dec 18   Jubilee of Liverpool University celebrated over three days (*see photo of 'Rag Week'*)

Left: This group of fancy dressed students from Liverpool University is collecting for the 'Students Hospital Collection' in 'Rag Week' 1931 - they were loaned the lorry by 'S Reece & Sons - wholesale dairymen'

Below: This aerial view shows the signs for the 'Belfast Express Steamers, Belfast' with 'Riverside Railway Station' to the right - Prince's dock is behind and directly behind that is the Liverpool Overhead Railway

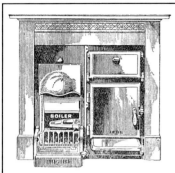

*Left: Tramcar No.587 is pictured at Pier Head in the early 1930s - this Dick Kerr 64 seater went into service in 1914 and was withdrawn in 1949 - this Route No.4 was bound for **Wavertree***

Below: The archway shield under construction at the main Liverpool entrance to the Mersey Tunnel in the old Haymarket

- Otterspool Park opened - 17 acres and cost £26,479[APOP]
- Health Centre opened in Knowsley Road, **Bootle**, serving the northern half of the borough - Balliol Road served the southern half

Jan 7   Liverpool City Council approved the purchase of 1,700 acres of land at **Knowsley** from Lord Derby - cost £185,000[LDPCE]

Feb 27   Liverpool Finance Committee decided to recommend to the City Council to seek powers to provide for the excess cost of the Mersey Tunnel estimated at £1,575,000[LDPCE]

Feb 29   Two large warehouses of the Blue Funnel Line destroyed by fire - damage estimated at £60,000

Apr 1   The boundaries of the County Borough of Liverpool extended to include the Township of **Speke**

Apr 9   Opening of the Marine Gardens, **Waterloo**

Apr 22   Trafalgar Dock with new graving dock and two bascule bridges opened by the Lady Mayoress

May   **Everton** FC 1st Division Champions for 1931/32

June 21   The Liverpool and Samaritan Hospital for Women opened by HRH the Duke of York and the Duchess

June 25   *Georgic (II)* maiden voyage to New York (*see photo*)

July 23   Statue of Eros, a replica of Sir Alfred Gilbert's work in London, unveiled in **Sefton** Park by the Lord Mayor

Oct 1   Christ Church, **Norris Green** consecrated

October   An extension to the School for the Blind opened - cost £24,000

Above Top: *The liner* Georgic (II) *was the last liner built for White Star. Launched 12 November 1931, her maiden voyage from Liverpool to New York was 25 June 1926. During the Second World War she became a troop ship but was bombed 14 July 1941 and rebuilt. She was scrapped in 1956*

Above: *This Liverpool Corporation, single-decker Karrier bus, pictured outside Edge Lane Works with 'Football' route indicators, was one of seven of this type which came into service in 1928 and only lasted five years, all being withdrawn 1933*

Above: *This postcard of Otterspool Park was sent in 1932 - the year it opened. Covering 17 acres, it had a fanciful pavilion with balcony, eight tennis courts, putting green and bowling green, with entertainments in summer[APOP]*

Right: *Liverpool Corporation Tram No.32 is proceeding down Church Street and about to pass one coming the other way - between the two, in front of the large Coopers building on the corner of Paradise Street, is a Crosville double-decker bus*

1933

Apr   New road 27 miles long from **Walton** Hall Avenue to **Swinton** opened. It was officially opened by the King & Queen on 18 July 1934, the same day as the Mersey Tunnel

May 27   The Princess Royal visited the ex-servicemen's exhibition in Bluecoat Chambers - also presented colours to the Lancashire Girl Guides' County Association on Aintree Racecourse

June   **Everton** FC winners of the FA Cup

June 3   **Bootle** Stadium opened - described as one of the finest sports grounds in the country - it provided work for the local unemployed

June 5   Foundation stone laid for the Roman Catholic Metropolitan Cathedral of Christ the King

July 2   The Municipal Airport at **Speke** officially opened by the Marquess of Londonderry, Secretary of State for Air with the greatest Air Pageant outside Hendon (London) being staged with 246 aircraft and 100,000 visitors (*see article this page*)

July 5   The Philharmonic Hall, Hope Street, destroyed by fire

July 21   The Liverpool University School of Architecture opened by Lady Leverhulme

Sept 23   *Royal Court Theatre* seriously damaged by fire

Oct 2   The President of the Board of Education (Lord Irwin) opened the Elementary School Teachers' Training College at **Ormskirk** (*see Edge Hill College* 1908)

Oct 4   HRH Prince George opened the extended and renovated Walker Art Gallery

Nov 14   The SS *Architect* went aground on the Plessington Bank in the River Mersey (*see photo*)

Dec 17   Over 34,000 people took advantage of the opportunity to inspect the Mersey Tunnel[LDPCE]

*Liverpool Corporation bought the 2,000 acre **Speke** Estate - with 418 acres for Speke Airport - work began in 1930. Imperial Airways operated an Argosy service between Liverpool, Manchester, Birmingham and Croydon being subsidised by the local authorities but lasted only three months - the aerodrome continued to be used solely by the flying club. An airport manager was appointed in 1932 with only 221 passengers using the airport - however in 1933 the number was over 3,600 - farm buildings were used as the terminal building and control tower*

Left: *The nearest Tramcar, No.369, was built in 1901 with an open top which was covered in 1905 and withdrawn from service in 1936 - pictured in South Castle Street, the new tram behind, No.770, was built in 1933 and withdrawn in 1953 - this was one of the original 'Green Godesses'*

Below: *The* Architect *is seen aground in low water on Pluckington Bank, in the River Mersey, on 14 November 1923 - the Mersey Dock and Harbour Board vessel* Salvor *is seen alongside the stricken vessel*

Left: This Liverpool Tramcar on Route No.11, is passing Rushworth & Draper's store, heading for Green Lane, **Stoneycroft**

Above: *Liverpool Corporation Tramcar No.234 on Route No.7 for Calderstones seen at Liverpool Pier Head*

Below: This shows Pitt Street bedecked with flags and bunting - this was the original 'Chinatown' before being re-established in the Great George Street area, its present site, following bombing by enemy aircraft during the May Blitz on 1941 - any excuse and the street was beautifully decorated

1934

Feb 9   Cunard and White Star shipping lines merged to become Cunard -White Star[LDPCE]

Mar 14   Midland & Scottish Air Ferries Ltd offered new destinations from Liverpool and Hooton Airports (*see advert opposite*)

Apr 3   Over 266,500 people took advantage of the four days opportunity to walk through the Mersey Tunnel[LDPCE]

Apr 7   Fire at garage at the junction of Lightbody Street and Great Howard Street - 40 loaded motor wagons destroyed

July   Mr HL Cohen gave £100,000 to Liverpool University for a new library

July 18   HM The King accompanied by HM The Queen opened the Queensway Mersey Tunnel (*see photo opposite*) he also opened the East Lancashire Road, the **Walton** Hall Park - and the new **Birkenhead** Library

Above: The caption on this 1930s comic postcard from Liverpool showing a distorted Liver Building photograph says "If you see Liverpool like this - then you're drunk"

Above: Queen Victoria's Monument is seen in Castle Street with the Midland Bank to the right and in the distance is the Town Hall - a horse and cart on the left is heading towards two trams coming from the right

Above: Looking down Lime Street, St Luke's Church is in the distance and the Washington Hotel is to the right - the tram in the centre seems to be following a horse & cart

BY AIR FOR BUSINESS AND PLEASURE

PHONES :
HOOTON   197
GARSTON   1041

Midland & Scottish Air Ferries now offer greater facilities for air travel in the British Isles and connect with continental air lines at Croydon. Why not fly ?

COMMENCING 14th March
* London to Belfast (via Birmingham, Liverpool and I.O.M.)
* Glasgow to London (via Liverpool and Birmingham.
* Glasgow — Campbeltown — Belfast.
   * (All twice daily in both directions).
† Glasgow — Campbeltown — Islay.
   † (Thrice weekly in both directions).
Glasgow to Stornoway (to commence late Spring).

Particulars cf Times, Fares and Special Charters from all travel agencies.

TRAVEL BY
MIDLAND & SCOTTISH
AIR FERRIES LTD.
Hooton Park Aerodrome and Liverpool Airport
Head Office :—RENFREW AERODROME, GLASGOW.
Also at BELFAST, BIRMINGHAM, ISLE-OF-MAN, LONDON.

Facts about the Mersey Tunnel: The road tunnel between Liverpool and Birkenhead under the River Mersey was one of the greatest feats of 'modern' engineering:- Begun: December 1925; Opened: July 1934; Cost: £7,723,000; Length of Tunnels: 2.62 miles; Width: main tunnel for four lanes of traffic - 36 feet, Branch tunnels for two lanes of traffic - 18 ft.; Internal diameter: 44 ft. and external 46 ft. 3 in.; Area of the cross section 1,680 sq. ft.; Total excavation: 1,200,000 tons, maximum quantity of water pumped out during construction was 4,300 gallons per minute

A mass of people wait for the Royal procession - which is seen on the right with King George V accompanied by Queen Mary - about to open the Mersey Tunnel on 18 July 1934

1935

Jan 31   New Air Mail and passenger service opened between **Speke** Airport, Liverpool and the Isle of Man

May 6   King George V Silver Jubilee

June 22   New St Andrew's Gardens municipal flats opened by Sir Kingsley Wood, Minister of Health

Sept 8   The Old Courthouse at **West Derby**, built in 1662, scheduled as an ancient monument

Sept 16   Three wooden water towers at Lister Drive Power Station destroyed by fire

Oct   Bouts-James Line inaugurated a twice-weekly fast cargo steamer service between Liverpool and Belfast

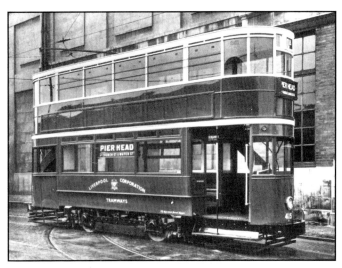

Above left: Liverpool Corporation Tramcar No.415, in operation from 1930 to 1950, pictured in front of the Edge Lane works

Above right: The Cheshire Lines Railway bridge at **Norris Green** is in the background, behind the No.616 Tramcar with a Clayton Square destination sign

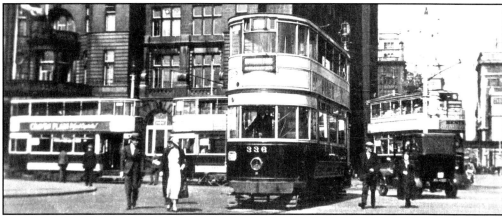

Above: Seen at Pier Head, Liverpool Corporation Tram No.336 which is on Route 6a from Bowring Park to Pier Head - it changed from this red and cream livery to green and cream in 1936 - it was destroyed in the Green Lane Depot fire of 1947

Left: This was a postcard showing the Floral Clock - whose cuckoo chimes interested young and old - in **Woolton** Wood which was described as being "an old English Garden, a natural beauty seldom seen so near to a large city" - it was opened in 1917

Above: Calderstones Park was named after the prehistoric Calderstones
[now preserved in the County Museum]
this shows the sundial in the park

LIVERPOOL GAS COMPANY

118 Years of Public Service

GAS

Throughout the reign of five monarchs. The Liverpool Gas Company has given continuous and never-failing service. By good will and traditional courtesy the Company has entrenched itself securely in the confidence of its consumers, until to-day it supplies gas to a population of over one million.

GAS THE FIRST CHOICE OF THE PUBLIC

HEAD OFFICES and SHOWROOMS . DUKE STREET.

Telephone . . Royal 4100

Right: This postcard sent in 1935 shows the queue of motor and horse-drawn vehicles for the luggage boats moored at the Liverpool Landing Stage - the Prenton *on the left and* Leasowe *on the right - one of the vehicles on board the* Prenton *is a Shell Petrol Wagon*

Above: Viewed from St George's plateau - Duke of Wellington's Column is on the left and the Empire Theatre *on the right advertising 'Billy Cotton & His Band' - which was later a favourite radio show*

91

1936

Jan 20   King George V died

Aug 17   An explosion occurred at the premises of the Atlas Oil and Tallow refinery, Naylor Street, Liverpool

Oct 20   Cunard White Star liner *Lancastria* went aground in the Mersey

Dec 11   King Edward renounces the throne and Duke of York then to be King[LDPCE]

Above: This advertising postcard for the 'Kohlers - Alfredo's' is signed on the back and says "Stadium Circus Liverpool Season 1936-37"

Right: This unusual view is of two men cleaning one of the two Liver Birds on top of the Liver Building

Above: This aerial view showing the Head Offices of the White Star Line and proximity to the principal railway stations and landing stage - the head office is the white building in James Street and shows Lime Street Station top right; Central Station below it and a sign pointing towards Exchange Station (middle left) - the Liverpool Overhead Railway is seen in front of the White Star offices running from left to right

Above: Looking up Ranelagh Street, with Church Street off to the left, the Adelphi Hotel *is the building at the top facing down. The sign for Lewis's store is seen above and behind the tram - Central Station entrance is on the right*

Right: Trinity Church Bootle, which is seen in Hawthorne Road, was built at the corner of Trinity Road in 1887

Below: Rex and Dora, the two lions pictured here with their trainer, were one of the attractions at the Liverpool Zoological Park and Gardens in Mossley Hill

Above: Woolton Convalescent Home was originally built in Hillfoot Road for Napoleanic prisoners of war, who planted the avenue of trees in Woolton Road leading to Garston

1937

- Higsons Brewery Ltd floated as a public company
- **Speke** Airport new control tower opened[RR&FofL]
- **Knotty Ash** Brewery was taken over by Higsons Brewery Ltd with over 70 public houses[WHATBG]

May 12   King George VI crowned

July 7   HRH Prince Chichibu of Japan visited Liverpool

July 20   New Borough of **Crosby** formed out of the Urban Districts of **Waterloo-with-Seaforth** and **Great Crosby**

Sept 1   Exchange buildings and Exchange Flags - demolition commenced

Sept 10   Minister of Labour visited Liverpool to inspect the various centres of Unemployed Social Welfare

Oct 4   The Harwich-Liverpool express jumped the rails and ripped way 60 - 80 yards of No.1 platform of Liverpool Central Station

Oct 5   The Minister of Health opened the combined Maternity & Child Welfare & School Medical Centre and inspected a number of housing sites

Oct 11   Sir Oswald Moseley, leader of the British Fascist Movement, was stoned at an open-air meeting in Liverpool and had a minor operation in hospital[LDPCE]

Oct 31   First Mass held in the Chapel of the Seven Dolours at the new Roman Catholic Cathedral, one of the two Crypt Chapels

Above: These two trams are pictured in Renshaw Street - the left Tramcar No.321 is on its way to Pier Head and was in service from 1922 until 1951

Above: One of the famous 'Bamforth' comic postcards with a local theme

Above: Looking up Lord Street with Horne Brothers, men's outfitters, pictured on the left on the corner of Paradise Street

Above: Parker Street with mainly tramcars in view - Jaeger's shop and Reeces' Cafe are on the left

Left: Looking to the left of the Overhead Railway the Dock Offices, Cunard and Liver Buildings can be seen, as can the Mersey Tunnel ventilation building - on the right is the Goree Piazzas - a scene that changed a few years later following the German air-raids

Above: This aerial view shows the Liverpool Overhead Railway running behind the Dock Offices, Cunard and Liver Buildings with Pier Head and landing stage in front

Right: The single-deck tram (second from left) was a German car, dating back to 1898, which was used to collect cash paid by conductors - mainly pennies and very heavy

Below: The snow has been cleared for the trams in Lord Street and this Liverpool Corporation Tramcar No.183 on route No.22a can proceed - Coopers' store can be seen to the left of the tram on the corner of Paradise Street and Kodak's shop to the right of the the tram

Above: Liverpool Corporation Tramcar No.947 is pictured on Route No.15 to **Croxteth** Road at Princes Avenue - this Streamliner 78 seater tram was in service from 1937 to 1946

1938

Feb 4   The 'Maritime Hall' for the National Union of Seamen opened in Canning Place

May 19   King George VI and Queen Elizabeth visited Liverpool to present colours to the Liverpool Scottish and the 5th Battalion King's Regiment (Liverpool) - also witnessing a display by children at **Wavertree** Playground

May 21   The Harold Cohen Library opened in Liverpool University

Sept   Main branch **Huyton** Library opened

Sept 11 A new figurehead representing Nelson was unveiled by the Poet Laureate John Masefield

Oct 13   The re-built *Royal Court Theatre* was opened

Oct 18   The Clarence Dock Electric Power Station opened

Nov 30   The Walter Harding Gymnasium opened at Liverpool University by Lord Derby, the Chancellor

Dec 10   **Formby** by-pass opened (*see photo*)

Above: Tramcar No.772 on the Outer Circular Route No.26 is seen in South Castle Street and behind is No.774 Tramcar on Route No.27 which went round the circular in the opposite direction

Left: Queen Victoria's Monument is pictured on the right with Austin Reed's Men's Outfitter's shop on the left - Lord Street is straight ahead

Right: Work started on the new Liverpool-Southport County Road A565 Formby by-pass on 9 April 1937 and was officially opened by the Earl of Derby on 10 December 1938 - this picture shows the southerly portion of the by-pass under construction - the total length was four miles and estimated cost £195,463[FBPOOB]

Left: Liverpool Corporation Tramcar No.342 on Route No.49 in Smithdown place, came into service in 1932 and was withdrawn in 1951 - note that this photograph was taken in April 1940 and due to the black-out, the kerb stones are painted black and white and the tram has a white bumper at the front

Right: Some two years after this photograph was taken in Church Street we would be at war with Germany and the City of Liverpool would be changed forever - Tram No.779 with Route No.14 on the left and Tram No.787, Route No.12 on the right - the Liver Birds on top of the Liver building can be seen above the building ahead

1939

- **Seaforth** Library, Crescent Road opened
- **Speke** Airport terminal building completed

Jan 2   West **Allerton** Station opened on the LMS Railway line[ISOLRS]

Jan 7   HMS *Liverpool* visited Liverpool

Jan 9   The 'Liverpool Shipwreck and Humane Society' celebrated its centenary

Apr 28   Commons approve conscription into the forces[LDPCE]

May   **Everton** FC 1st Division Champions 1938/39

June 17   The new Cunard-White Star liner *Mauretania* sailed from Liverpool on her maiden voyage to New York

June 19   The New Philharmonic Hall in Hope Street opened (*see photo on opposite page*)

July 3   **Garston** Church Road Station closed on the LMS Railway line[ISOLRS]

July 7   Statues of King George V and Queen Mary unveiled at the entrance to the Mersey Tunnel by HRH the Duke of Kent

Aug 23   The Minister of War Transport formerly appointed the Port Emergency Committee representing all aspects of the working of the docks[PAW]

Sept 3   **War declared**

Above: Liverpool Corporation Tram No.120 is standing at the Seaforth Regent Road termini - this was a Dick Kerr tram built in 1929 and withdrawn in 1948 - the enquiry office on the right was once the gatehouse of Seaforth Horse Tram Depot

*Left: Liverpool Corporation Tram No.386 is seen in St Helens Road, **Prescot** in June 1939 - already the kerb stones and posts have been painted black and white for the black-out*

*Below: This aerial view of **Huyton** shows how the old village looked before being altered in the 1960s - the Parish Church is in the centre background (see also 1860 before the cross was moved)*

Left: *Cars are parked in the middle of Lime Street when parking was not a problem in the centre of Liverpool - the Imperial Hotel & Restaurant is seen on the right - St Luke's Church is in the background which is beyond the Adelphi Hotel whose building towers above all others on the left*

Above: The black granite column is seen above the rear of St George's Hall - it was part of the design of the Mersey Tunnel which opened in 1934 - cars on the right are paying at the toll booths while a Mersey Tunnel Policeman is by his motor bike in the foreground

Right: *The new Philharmonic Hall in Hope Street was built to replace the old Hall which was burnt down in 1933 - the screen set and organ console rose from a chamber below when required - the shell-shaped structure accommodated over 1,750 people*

1940

May 1   King George VI and Queen Elizabeth visited Merseyside[PAW]

May 11   Mr Churchill to be the new Prime Minister[LDPCE]

May 31   Dunkirk evacuation[LDPCE]

Aug 1   First bombs fell in the Liverpool area on **Halewood** - no casualties[BOM]

Aug 17   First bombs on Liverpool fell in the Caryl Street area, **Toxteth** - damage to the Overhead Railway[BOM]

Aug 28   Over 150 enemy aircraft attacked Merseyside with incendiaries and high-explosive bombs including the city but most damage was done to residential and private property - **Mossley Hill** Church was badly damaged[BOM]

Aug 31   Three raids using incendiaries and HE bombs - the Custom House and two cotton warehouses set on fire - an air-raid shelter received a direct hit and an adjoining RAF balloon site destroyed killing all personnel[MAW]

Aug   Civilian toll: Liverpool 37 killed - **Bootle**: no deaths[BOM]

Sept 3   During two raids - parachute flares, incendiaries and HE bombs fell on the **Kensington** district, the Ullet Road area, Lark Lane and **Aigburth Vale** - incendiaries set fire to a Rope Works at Lodge Lane, a girl's High School at **Aigburth** and Pollard's Garage severely damaged[MAW] (*see photo page 102*)

Sept   Visit to Liverpool by the Duke of Kent

Sept 4   Damage was caused to: **Edge Hill** Goods Station; Lister Drive Power Station; the Dunlop Rubber Works; the Tunnel Road Cinema; an ice-skating rink; a nearby billiards hall and the Green Lane area including a surface shelter, fire station, several schools and churches[MAW]

Sept 5   HE bombs and incendiaries fell on the Cladia Street, **Walton** area, Washington Street and St James Road were also badly damaged - crude oil-type bombs were used for the first time causing extensive damage to houses - incendiaries set fire to the **Everton** FC seating[MAW]

Sept 11   **West Derby** and **Woolton** areas attacked with HE bombs; houses in the **Speke** area severely damaged[MAW]

Sept 17   The bombing raid over **Garston** and **Speke** narrowly missed the Rootes aircraft factory - bombs landed on Green Lane **Old Swan** area, demolished a house killing eight Auxiliary Firemen[MAW]

Sept 18   Over 1,000 HE bombs and 500 incendiaries were dropped over a large area of Liverpool - railway lines were damaged at **Brownlow Hill** and St Michael's Station, **Aigburth** - work stopped at the ATM works **Old Swan** due to an unexploded bomb[MAW]

Sept 21   Raids over the city seriously damaged TJ Hughes store in London Road - Central Station and the Mersey Underground received direct hits and two trains were seriously damaged - large fires broke out in the Alexandra Dock warehouses and a timber yard was set on fire in Rimrose Road[MAW]

Sept 23   **Bootle** suffered considerable damage from the first attack; **Walton** received the brunt of the second and the third attack included 'Molotov Bread Baskets' being used for the first time with the church in Robson Street being damaged[MAW]

Sept 24   The Germans changed the time of their attack to early morning and used a new type of Magnesium bomb - The city centre was targeted with shops in Parker Street, Clayton Square and Church Street set on fire - The Stanley Tobacco Warehouse and Silcock's Cattle Food Mill in Great Howard Street and Love Lane received direct hits[MAW]

Sept 25   Duke of Kent visited Liverpool[PAW]

Sept 26   Extensive damage was caused to the Wapping, King's Queen's, Coburg and Brunswick Docks - 13 warehouses were seriously damaged - the MD & HB Offices and Cunard Buildings were hit by HE bombs - at one government building all the tax records were completely destroyed[MAW]

Sept 27   Houses in Great Homer Street were demolished and the Council School in Banks Road, **Garston** damaged[MAW]

Sept 28   Main areas damaged were the **Dingle, Aigburth** and **Everton** areas - the Hamlet Free Church at **Aigburth** was destroyed by an oil bomb which also caused damage to the *Mayfair Cinema* and **Aigburth** Public Library - two firemen were killed at Duke's Dock[MAW]

Sept   Civilian toll: Liverpool 221 killed - **Bootle**: 28[BOM]

Oct 7   Severe damage to houses in Stanley Road, Great Mersey Street, Lichfield Road and the **Wavertree** area[MAW]

Oct 9   Ernest Bevin MP, Minister of Labour, visited Liverpool

Oct 10   Damage caused to a children's sanatorium; the Ritz Roller Skating Rink at Catharine Street; houses in **Everton** Valley; Mill Street; Marmington Road, **Anfield** and Hogarth Road, **Kirkdale**[MAW]

Oct 11   Severe damage caused to property in the city - South John Street; James Street; Red Cross Street; Paradise

Above: *The ship that the fighter planes were sent from America in, is moored at Princes Landing Stage*

Street; Hanover Street and South Castle Street - also damage to the dock sheds, the Harbour Master's House, 4 ships, Alexandra and Langdon Docks[MAW]

Oct 13   Forty enemy bombers attacked - 11 people were killed and nine seriously injured in a large block of tenements at Myrtle Gardens - houses damaged in Gadsby Street **Everton**; fires at dock sheds in North Hornby and Gladstone Docks[MAW]

Oct 14   Monday - raids most evenings during this week[MAW]

Oct 21   Monday - raids across the city most evenings - including the introduction of the 'screaming bomb'[MAW]

Oct 28   Monday - it was clear that the Germans were concentrating their efforts on the Port Installations[MAW]

Oct 29   The Bryant & May match factory at **Garston** set alight[MAW] (*see photo on next page*)

Oct   Civilian toll: Liverpool 106 killed - **Bootle**: 10[BOM]

Nov   Was a relatively 'quiet' month compared with October - until the 28/29th:-

Nov 28   This was to be the worst raid experienced up until then when Merseyside was the main target - for seven and a half hours wave after wave of bombers devastated Merseyside with their incendiary and HE bombs - including the introduction of the 'parachute' or 'land' mine where the bomb was released and drifted down on a parachute, causing more devastation when it hit the ground than the conventional bomb. Widespread devastation was caused with many areas, particularly around the docks, being alight - in one incident where a bomb fell on a school shelter at Durning Road, 180 were killed[BOM] (*see photo on page 102*)

Nov 29   First full scale bombing attack on the Port of Liverpool - the main attack lasted over 2.5 hours during which time over 200 people were killed

Nov   Civilian toll: Liverpool 305 killed - **Bootle**: 6[BOM]

Dec 18   King George VI and Queen Elizabeth visited Liverpool (*see photo*)

Dec 20   December had been free from attacks until 50 bombers attacked the city for nine and a half hours - 42 people died when a bomb destroyed an unofficial shelter under Bentwick Street railway arches - nine men were killed at Waterloo Dock - St Nicholas' Church destroyed by enemy action, only the walls and vestries survived. It was rebuilt [see October 1952]

Dec 21   This was an even bigger raid with over 150 bombers - the following Northern docks were seriously damaged:- Canada; Gladstone; Brocklebank, Princes; Wapping; King's and Carriers - havoc was caused throughout the city[MAW]

Dec 22   The raids continued for the next two days - including Christmas Eve with many more casualties[MAW]

Dec   Civilian toll: Liverpool 412 killed - **Bootle**: 108[BOM]

Above: Pollards Garage, Ullet Road destroyed after a bombing raid 5 September 1940

Above: *King George VI & Queen Elizabeth visited Liverpool to meet the people 1 May 1940 - King George returned in November*

Above: *Winston Churchill paid many visits to Liverpool during the war to keep up the moral of the population who suffered at the hands of the German bombers*

Above: *This burnt-out shell is all that remained after a bombing raid at the Robinson Cleaver premises in Church Street*

Above: *This was the scene after Durning Road School was struck by a landmine - 180 people were killed in the shelter*

Above: *Bryant and May's burnt out factory following a bombing raid on **Bootle***

T.S. ST. SEIRIOL

Photo of plaque in saloon entrance inscribed with message received from Minister of Shipping expressing admiration of courage and endurance of Master and Crew at Dunkirk evacuation.

COPYRIGHT, TIERNEY   ST. GEORGE BLDS., LIVERPOOL, I

Above: *Postcard of the Liverpool – Llandudno TS St Seriol and plaque above inscribed with a message from the Minister of Shipping expressing admiration of courage and endurance of Master and Crew at the Dunkirk evacuation - dated 17 June 1940*

Right: *Preparations had been in hand since November 1938 regarding the evacuation of children from areas in the country of high-risk from German bombing which included Liverpool, Birkenhead and Wallasey. From 1 to 5 September 1939 thousands of children were evacuated from Liverpool mainly to the less vulnerable area of Wales. Many returned over the following months due to the 'phoney war' but once the Germans started bombing Merseyside in August 1940, thousands of children were sent on ships to the safe shores of Canada.*

On 13 September 1940 the City of Benares *(see photo) set sail from Liverpool bound for Canada with 400 people on board including 100 children. The ship was initially escorted by a Naval destroyer on the dangerous part of the voyage but after four days the escort left them. The German submarine U-48 torpedoed the* City of Benares *on 17 September and 262 people on board lost their lives with only 13 children surviving[CoB]*

"Children of Benares" by David Roberts - e-mail: www.avidpublications.co.uk

•   Linacre Lane Branch Library opened in **Bootle**

Jan 8   Approximately 200 bombers attacked the Liverpool area - although the number of casualties was light[MAW]

Jan   Civilian toll: Liverpool 43 killed - **Bootle**: no deaths[BOM]

Feb   Civilian toll: Liverpool two killed - **Bootle**: no deaths[BOM]

Mar 12   Heavy attack - 126 fires dealt with in Liverpool using fire brigades from other areas

Mar 13   An intense bombing raid killed six firemen in Liverpool - a Heinkel 111 bomber shot down over Liverpool by a night fighter - at least 270 incendiary bombs fell on the **Speke** district setting fire to houses and damaging the aircraft factory[MAW]

March   Civilian toll: Liverpool 101 killed - **Bootle**: no deaths[BOM]

Apr 7   Despite a six hour raid there were few casualties - two of the 75 enemy planes were shot down[MAW]

Apr 25   Winston Churchill, the Prime Minister, visited Liverpool docks[PAW]

April   Civilian toll: Liverpool 31 killed - **Bootle**: no deaths[BOM]

May 1   The first of eight continuous nights of bombing which became known as the 'May Blitz'[MAW]

May 2   The most sensational single incident of the war occurred when a barrage balloon fell onto the deck of the Brocklebank steamer the SS *Malakand* which lay in Huskisson Dock No.2 and contained 1,000 tons of shells and bombs due for the Middle East and immediately burst into flames. The fire was kept under control for almost four hours when the first of many explosions occurred. Part of the ship's plates were recovered 2.5 miles away and the four ton anchors were blown 100 yards. Only four people were killed which was astonishing considering the amount of destruction. Despite the damage, the port returned to normal quite quickly[POWL] six enemy aircraft were brought down

Above: Ranelagh Street completely covered in debris following a bombing raid - Lewis's store is on the right and the Adelphi Hotel *beyond*

Above: This damage was caused to houses in Ballantyne Road in **West Derby** *following an air raid on 26 April 1941*

Above: From the outset of war, Littlewoods offered the Government their vast organisation to help the war effort - this factory in Liverpool produced parachutes - by the end of the war Littlewoods had made over 5 million

Above: This was all that was left of Evans Medical who were in Hanover Street and Seel Street on 3 May 1941 following the German raid

May 3   Heaviest raid over Merseyside from early evening to dawn - large fires ranged from the North End of the docks to **Dingle** in the south - 100s were killed and injured - **Mossley Hill** Hospital received a direct hit from an HE bomb with casualties remarkably light - other buildings hit this night were Lewis's Stores (*see photo*), the Museum, the Bluecoat Chambers, the Technical College and the *Rotunda Theatre* - on this raid the Germans used 10 inch foil strips for the first time, to disrupt the radar defences[MAW]

May 4   Light raids on the 4, 5 & 6 May

May 5   Canada Dock Station closed on the London Midland & Scottish Railway line following enemy action

May 7   Severe damage caused to the docks

May 14   A mass funeral held at **Anfield** Cemetery where 1,000 victims of the 'May Blitz' were buried in a common grave[MAW]

May   The 'May Blitz' will never be forgotten by those who lived through it - 6,000 people were accommodated away from the devastated areas in Liverpool and **Bootle** - 'Chinatown', was forced to move away from an area nearer the docks and was re-established in the Great George Square area, where it remains to this day

May   Civilian toll: Liverpool 1,453 killed - **Bootle**: 257[BOM]

Oct 18   King George VI and Queen Elizabeth visited Liverpool[PAW]

Above: the extent of the bomb damage can be seen from this aerial view of Lord Street and South Castle Street

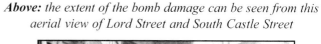

Above: Custom House pub rescuers following a bombing raid in October 1940

Above top: Only the main entrance of the Cotton Exchange remained after the German bombing raid

Above: South Castle Street after a week of suffering from German raids

Left: Rimrose Road Bootle showing the effects of landmines - rows of houses once stood on this site with only the brick-built shelters still seen standing

Jan 10   Last bomb to fall on Merseyside

April 9   King Haakon of Norway visited Liverpool and told Liverpool dockers that "your job perhaps is not as glamorous as that of soldiers and naval men, but it is just as important"[PAW]

Nov 8   Mrs Roosevelt, the US President's wife, toured Liverpool mainly to visit the USA troops[PAW]

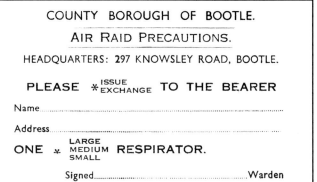

COUNTY BOROUGH OF BOOTLE.

AIR RAID PRECAUTIONS.

HEADQUARTERS: 297 KNOWSLEY ROAD, BOOTLE.

PLEASE ✻ ISSUE EXCHANGE TO THE BEARER

Name..

Address......................................

ONE ✕ LARGE MEDIUM SMALL RESPIRATOR.

Signed.............................Warden

Group   Sector No. ....

✻ Please strike out Words not applicable.

Above: The worshippers at St Nicholas' Church view the damage caused by the German bombers in December 1940 but were able to attend a service in part of the Church not badly damaged - the church was restored after the war

Above: This AEC Regent Mk 1 bus Reg. No.DKC650 is seen in wartime livery with mudguards and side bottom rail both painted white so the bus could be seen in the black-out

Above Left: Liverpool Corporation Tram No.902 is seen in St Oswalds Street before double track was laid from Edge Lane - taken during wartime with white bumpers, poles were also painted white - behind the second pole from the left painted on the wall is "Bacon 1/3d per pound" and a quote "War Makes Rich Richer Poor Poorer"

Left: Liverpool Corporation Tram No.771 can be seen at Pier Head with white bumpers, anti-blast netting over the windows and headlamp mask

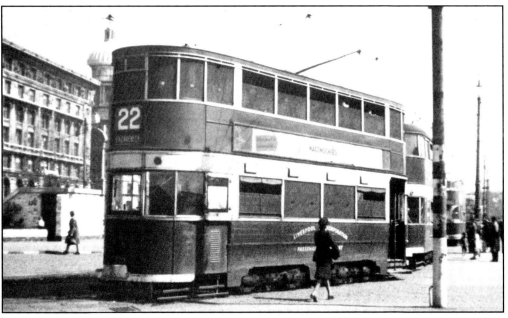

1943

- Longview Branch Library, **Huyton** opened
- July   Lever Bros. set up the Lifeboat Emergency Bath Service and National Emergency Washing Service which had been used following the bombing on Merseyside utilising two Rinso demonstration vans - further vans were ordered and by July 1943 there was a fleet of 10 - five of these were used to bath 10,000 Italian prisoners of war from North Africa in three days who disembarked at Liverpool

*Above: This multi-view postcard of **Waterloo** was posted 1943*

Above: This Leyland Titan bus was one of 84 old London buses acquired by Liverpool Corporation in 1940, mainly to carry workers to the Kirkby munitions factory

Right: These buses were converted into ambulances during the Second World War

Left: The newly-arrived body of an aeroplane having been loaded onto a trailer, is seen in front of the Liver Building, about to set off to be assembled.

*Liverpool was the main port for the American Convoys which included aircraft packed onto the decks of aircraft carriers and other vessels - in all some 73,000 planes and gliders were landed at the port. The former luggage boat Oxton was fitted with cranes to unload the planes from the ships in mid river by crane onto the deck of the Oxton which could take several planes - then transferred to the dock side where cranes lifted them straight onto low-loaders - this proved successful and two other former luggage boats were similarly converted - over 11,000 planes were landed in this way. They were then transported up the floating roadway and through the city - many of them going on to the aircraft factory at **Speke** where they would be assembled. The route to the airport had to be cleared in readiness for the large vehicles with some 70 tram standards and lamp posts plus over 100 trees and 50 traffic signs being moved[POW]*

Above: This Americam Army lorry is seen being unloaded onto the docks at Liverpool. Many of the vehicles brought over in 1943 were destined for the 'D' Day landings

Below: Another vehicle - this time a tank - being unloaded onto a low-loader on the docks at Liverpool, off a convoy vessel from America

Above: Dunlop Rubber advert - their factory in Liverpool received a direct hit from German bombers 4 September 1940. In February 1945, Dunlop leased the former Ministry of Aircraft Production 'Shadow' factory at Speke which had been used to make over 4,752 bombers, employing at its peak 9,600 people. Initially they manufactured cycle tubes; car and heavy transport tyres; footwear and aero brake components. Later a pilot plant was established to manufacture tennis balls followed by Dunlop boots; cycle saddles; cycle covers; golf balls; car tubes etc[LandIM]

1944

- A plaque was unveiled in the Port of Liverpool to commemorate the British and American unity of effort in the port by Lady Sefton, who was an American[PAW]
- July 12 Following the death of Captain FJ Walker DSO, who commanded the Atlantic Escort Fleet, a service was held at Liverpool Cathedral (*see photo and article*)
- Oct 18 German maps and booklets found in Belgium by Allied troops revealed that **Southport** was to be the centre of one of Hitler's 'invasion towns' and included other places within a wide radius[LDPCE]
- Oct Princess Juliana of the Netherlands inspected Dutch vessels in port at Liverpool[PAW]

Above: This plaque was unveiled in the Port of Liverpool to commemorate the British and American unity of effort in the port, by Lady Sefton, who was an American - the plaque read:-
"HERE IN THE DARK DAYS OF WAR AND IN THE DAWN OF VICTORY AMERICAN TROOPS AND CARGOES MOVED THROUGH THIS PORT FURTHERED BY BRITISH AND AMERICANS WORKING TOGETHER. THIS STONE RECORDS THEIR UNITY IN ACCOMPLISHING THEIR MISSION - ERECTED BY THE 15th PORT - USA - 1944
The group from the left was:- Admiral Sir Max Horton, Commander-in-Chief, Western Approaches; the Lord Mayor and Lady Mayoress of Liverpool (the Earl and Countess of Sefton); Sir Thomas AL Brocklebank, Chairman of the MD&HB and Col. HT Duffie, Port Commander, US Army, who gave the plaque [PAW]

Above: Captain FJ Walker DSO and two bars, who commanded the Atlantic Escort Force based in Liverpool, returning from a patrol where they sunk six U-Boats. He is seen coming ashore as a hero in March 1941 - it was thanks to his courage and genius that we overcame the 'U' Boat threat and triumphed in the battle of the Atlantic - he died from an illness four months later. Following a moving service at Liverpool Cathedral his coffin was borne down to the River Mersey and then onto a vessel before being buried at sea.
At the service the following quote was made
"Not dust, nor the light weight of a stone,
but all the sea of the Western Approaches shall be his tomb",

Below: Work on developing Speke industrial and housing estates continued in 1944 having been been put on hold when war broke out in 1939

Above: Martins Bank, who had over 600 branches, had its head office in Liverpool - they are advertising for new customers in the form of members of HM Forces or Civil Defence

- Peel Road Branch lending Library opened in **Bootle**[BOH]
- May 8 VE Day [victory in Europe] (*see photo*)
- June 3 The last convoy from America during the war was escorted into Liverpool by allied aircraft[PAW]
- Aug 15 VJ Day [victory in Japan]
- Oct Nursery for 22 children under five opened in **Bootle**[BOH]
- Nov It was announced that Liverpool's oldest Boer War veteran, Captain George Tilford had died aged 85[L45]
- Nov 29 **Crosby** Historical Society founded - to stimulate interest in the Borough of Crosby to research into its past and present history
- Dec The Cunard passenger tender *Skirmisher,* built in 1884, was scrapped
- Dec The Liverpool Housing Committee announced that 54 temporary pre-fab bungalows were ready for occupation and that work was proceeding on new houses at **Speke**[L45]

Above: Looking across the River Mersey, this was the scene following the spectacular firework celebrations operated from barges in the river, with the Liver Building seen on the right

Below: These pre-fabricated houses (known as pre-fabs) *are seen near completion in Townsend Avenue, Liverpool. Pre-fabs were erected from 1945 to ease the housing shortage following the destruction by enemy bombing of a large number of houses. The ones pictured had an entrance hall; kitchen; living room; bathroom with separate toilet; airing cupboard and two bedrooms. They were intended as a temporary measure with an expected life of five to ten years - some lasted for over 50 years*

Above: Despite it being 1945, Garlick, Burrell & Edwards were advertising Vauxhall cars priced from £290 + purchase tax and Bedford vans from £215 (no purchase tax as vans were exempt). They stated permits could be applied for to purchase the models listed and that all models would be in production by the end of the year (1945)

1946

- **Crosby** Carnival Week started again for the first time after the war - £4,459 raised for the Waterloo Hospital[BoCOG]

Apr 1   Liverpool Corporation started redeveloping the former Royal Ordnance Filling Factory at **Kirkby**, near Liverpool and half a mile from the East Lancashire Road, with the object of providing productive work for the local unemployed. Due to the shortage of building materials and the bomb damage to existing buildings in the city, businesses were glad to have ready-made premises - this was the start of the Kirkby Trading Estate. Before the war the Corporation had acquired about six square miles of land but when war broke out 750 acres of this site were developed by the Ministry of Supply as a monster shell and bomb-filling factory which was operating within nine months. By 1945, some 30,000 workers were employed here, the majority being women - but with the end of the war in sight there was no need for this factory so the employees were made redundant and the Corporation stepped in

July   Skytravel Limited became the first post-war independent charter company to be based at **Speke**[LA50A]

Aug 1   The state airline carrier, British European Airways, formed - they took over many of the previously independent Liverpool routes[LA50A]

Above: **Bootle** *Stadium, a 14 acre arena with covered stand, was opened in 1933 - home to Bootle FC, around the perimeter of the stadium was an athletics track which was also used for cycling events*
Below: The Bootle Municiple 18 hole Golf Course in Dunnings Bridge Road also had an 18 hole putting course and was home to **Bootle** *Golf Club*

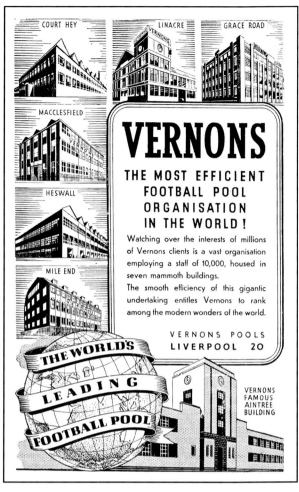

Above: Vernons Pools claimed to be the 'world's leading' and 'most efficient' whereas Littlewoods claimed to be 'the world's largest and best football pool' - Vernons pools were founded by Vernon Sangster in 1925

Below: Vernons Pools main premises are pictured in **Aintree**

Above: The horses and riders in the Grand National Steeplechase, held at Aintree, are seen at Beecher's Brook

- Three Civic Restaurants taken over by **Bootle** Corporation from the Ministry of Food:- 'Victoria', junction of Strand and Rimrose Roads; 'Derby' 376/380 Stanley Road and 'Mersey' 223 Stanley Road[BOM]
- Conversion from trams to buses approved with first stages begun in late 1947
- Work completed on a scheme in **Bootle** for 26 bungalows for the aged with gardens maintained by the Corporation[BOM]
- Work started on 850 temporary pre-fab houses allocated to **Bootle**[BOM](see 1945)

May   Liverpool FC Division 1 Champions 1946/47

June 16   **Garston** Dock Station closed on the London Midland & Scottish Railway line[ISOLRS]

*Above: St Katharine's College, pictured in Taggart Avenue, **Childwall**, Liverpool, had its foundings in **Warrington** in 1844 and was known as the Warrington Training College. The building was burnt down in 1923 and the college relocated to Battersea. They returned in 1930 to the new buildings pictured here and changed their name to St Katharine's College in 1938. A year later they were on the move again, this time evacuated to Kendal when the buildings were commandeered by the Northern Hospital - they returned in 1947 [today it is part of Liverpool Hope University]*

Left: The 1947 Hillman Minx was based on the 1940 model with post-war improvements. Powered by a 35 hp engine with 1184cc side valve engine - it was available from Kirbys of Liverpool

*Above: Liverpool Tramcar No.871 is seen on Route No.21 heading for **Aintree** - in the background is Hope Brothers, Tailors on the corner of Lord Street and Whitechapel*

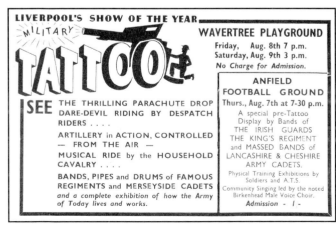

*Above: An advert for the Liverpool Military Tattoo at **Wavertree** Playground which was free - prior to which there was a pre-Tattoo display of bands at **Anfield** Football Ground*

1948

Feb 5   Death reported of Earl of Derby at **Knowsley** Hall[LDPCE]

Apr 1   The Liverpool Electricity Undertaking was taken over by the British Electricity Authority and distribution in the area was under thc control of the Merseyside & North Wales Electricity Board

May 31   The following stations closed on the LMS Railway line:- Alexandra Dock, **Bootle** Balliol Road, Breck Road, Edge Lane, Spellow, Stanley, **Tuebrook, Walton** & **Anfield**[ISOLRS]

Nov 12   Manx plane crashed in River Mersey with seven lives lost[LDPCE]

Above: Artist's bird's eye view of the Mills of J Bibby & Sons Ltd, Liverpool. The firm of J Bibby was founded in Lancaster c1878 and in 1885, the business was transferred to Liverpool finding all the facilities for rapid expansion in the Port. Initially the business was confined to seed-crushing and manufacture of cattle food. They expanded into the soap market then edible oil and fats. In 1948 they produced over 10,000 tons a week of cattle food and 1,500 tons of vegetable oil - employing over 3,000 people and running two experimental farms in Wirral

*Above: The Hag Plantation Site, **Huyton** was built partly by local contractors and partly by direct labour under the direction of the Engineers and Surveyors' Department of the Huyton UDC[HWRLGE]*

*Above: Derby Road **Huyton** looking north*

*Above: Derby Road **Huyton** looking south (see 1860)*

*Above: Speke Airport was described as being built on land of approximately 2,216 acres of land acquired from the **Speke** Estate but did not include the historic Speke Hall and grounds - situated six miles to the south-east of the city centre, it was opened in 1933[cofloh]*

- Population of Liverpool 802,000
- Blackledges, Bakers of **Bootle**, celebrate their centenary (*see advert on this page*)
- Crosby's first Festival of Music organised by **Crosby** Rotary Club[BoCOG]

Mar 21   Two people shot dead at a hold-up at the Cameo cinema [LDPCE]

Mar 29   Princess Elizabeth and the Duke of Edinburgh visited Liverpool to inaugurate the new **Waterloo** Dock and open the new doors of the Rankin Porch of the Anglican Cathedral[LCS]

May 19   Mr Churchill praised the courage and fortitude of the people of Liverpool during the war - at a banquet in the Town Hall[LDPCE]

Nov 10   Damage caused by the fire at South Gladstone Dock was estimated at £2,000,000[LDPCE]

Above: There are 10 trams and buses pictured in Lime Street of which only two seem to be trams - which eventually finished in Liverpool in 1957

Above: Liverpool Corporation Tram No.635 is pictured in Aigburth Road in its last summer of operation - having started in 1921 it was withdrawn in 1949

Left: James Blackledge's first shop opened in Fox Street in 1849 - however in this advert they are still coping with rationing four years after the war ended when they say "We hope present restrictions may soon be relaxed and as more materials become available, we look forward to being able to offer more varieties both in bread and in cakes" (see also 1908)

Left: Liverpool Corporation 'Streamliner' Tram No.968 on Route No.19 to Pier Head is seen on the East Lancashire Road - this tram started service in 1937 and was withdrawn in 1955. This route, opened in 1943, was the last to be laid, serving the Royal Ordnance Factory in Kirkby. The poles came from Coventry when the tramways were destroyed in air raids

1950

- Otterspool Promenade constructed
- Feb 8   George Kelly found guilty of the Cameo Cinema murder by a second jury[LDPCE]
- Feb 24   Reported that the Conservatives had regained a majority of the seats they had held in Liverpool since 1885 - with the exception of the previous four years[LDPCE]
- June 1   First UK passenger service by helicopter from **Speke** Airport to Cardiff with two Westland Sikorskys each carrying three passengers - after 10 months they were replaced by DH 89 Rapides[LA50A]

Above: Northern system of docks at Liverpool with the Liverpool Overhead Railway seen snaking its way at the right edge of the docks

GITTINS BROS.

Building Contractors

DERWENT ROAD—
PART OF ONE OF OUR
CONTRACTS FOR
CROSBY CORPORATION

Telephone : Gt. Crosby 3758

*Left: The houses in the Gittins Bros advert were some of those that the building contractor erected for **Crosby** Corporation after the war*

John Irwin Sons & Co Ltd in 1950 was 76 years old - when they produced a booklet *The Story of Irwins*. John Irwin opened his first shop in **Kirkdale** [see 1874] and by 1887 had 15 branches on Merseyside. He opened his first warehouse in Orwell Road which later expanded and included the offices. In 1892, the firm became John Irwin & Co Ltd, adopting all the most up-to-date ideas for ensuring food production and distribution under the finest hygienic conditions.

By 1950 Irwins had over 200 branches in North Wales, Lancashire, Cheshire and Shropshire; a large distribution depot in Orwell Road (*see photo*); modern food factories at Long Lane, **Aintree** & **Belle Vale** and employed almost 1,600 people. From the early days of horse-drawn wagons and steam wagons their transport had increased to 70 motor vehicles[TSOI]

Above: Irwin's Warehouse and offices in Orwell Road
Below: An Irwin's Store in 1950

Above: Bird's eye view of Pier Head with the circles in front of the Liver and Cunard buildings denoting the tram system with passengers having access to the ferries via the landing stage - damage caused by German bombing can be seen to the right with damaged buildings and derelict bomb sites

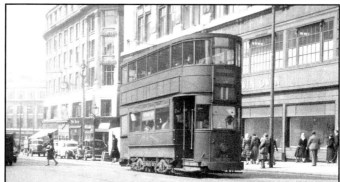

Above: This Route No.11 to Green Lane, Liverpool Corporation tram is looking very drab in grey wartime livery outside Owen Owen's store in Clayton Square - it came into service in 1930 and was withdrawn in 1950

Feb 15   Last trams in **Bootle** withdrawn[LTVol2]

Mar 5   **Otterspool** Station closed on the Cheshire Lines Committee line[ISOLRS]

Apr 2   Ford and Linacre Road Stations closed on the **Bootle - Aintree** Railway - line still open for goods[ISOLRS]

May 11   Mr Churchill to be the new Prime Minister[LDPCE]

July 14   The Walker Art Gallery re-opened after 12 years[LDPCE]

July 19   An important unit of the Home Fleet, including the Aircraft Carrier *Indomitable* in company with three destroyers and two frigates, arrived in Liverpool and stayed for a week. The public were able to view the ships during their visit[FOBb]

July 22   Start of the first week of 'Festival of Britain' celebrations[FOBb] (*this and next page*)

July 22   Chipperfields Circus and Zoo started their first performance at the Review Field, **Sefton Park** - the big top was the largest ever made in Great Britain, seating over 4,500 people - they performed here for two weeks[FOBb]

July 28   An exciting programme of small circuit motor cycle races held at **Altcar** Rifle Range[FOBb]

July 28   Port dock workers held a Sports Day at the **Seaforth** Stadium on Saturday, which included athletics, brass bands, a fun fair etc[FOBb]

July 29   Start of the second week of 'Festival of Britain'[FOBb]

Aug 4   The Liverpool Flying Club presented a spectacular air display of formation flying, aerobatics and dive bombing carried out by many types of aircraft, including the most modern jet fighters of the RAF[FOBb]

Aug 6   Start of the third week of 'Festival of Britain'[FOBb]

Aug 11   A marathon race was run in and around the City finishing at the Liverpool **Anfield** Football ground[FOBb]

Nov 17   Princess Elizabeth and the Duke of Edinburgh received a warm welcome on their return from USA and Canada via Liverpool - they visited the Cathedral and heard the first peal of the newly hung bells[LDPCE]

Right: Finch Hall Estate was one of the new post-war townships shown in an idyllic setting

Above: The Stork Hotel incorporated the Festival of Britain logo in their advert

In 1947, the Government decided that the centenary of the Great Exhibition of 1851 should be marked by national displays. These would demonstrate to the world, the British advances in science, technology, industrial design, as well as the arts and architecture. Battersea Park in London was chosen as the centrepiece for the Festival, with displays in other cities around the United Kingdom - including Liverpool. The three-week festival officially started on 22 July and ended on 12 August (*see next page*)[FOBb]

*Above: In medieval times the villages of both **Great Crosby** and **Little Crosby** only had about 20 families in each village - in 1948, when this photograph was taken of Little Crosby, the total population of the Borough was 59,000[BoCOG]*

*Left: The Old St Michael's Well on **Crosby** Village Green still remains, although covered in and had a wooden cross erected over it. In olden days the Cross and Well were decorated each year with flowers on St Michael's Day (29 September), while games were played on the village green[BoCOG]*

1951

Liverpool Celebrated the Festival of Britain

Entertainment at the theatre included:- performances from the Covent Garden Opera; English Opera Group; Saddler's Wells Ballet; The Old Vic Theatre Company; Liverpool Playhouse Company; Royal Philharmonic Orchestra; London Philharmonic Orchestra; Liverpool Philharmonic Orchestra etc.

Some of the entertainment included:- at least 12 brass bands performed in the city during the festival; lunch-time concerts were given in a special arena at Lord Street on a site adjoining the Industrial Exhibition; concerts were also given each evening, and weekend afternoons; at the Philharmonic Hall on each Friday evening there was a brass band and choral concert including the massed bands of the King's Regiment (Liverpool), the Irish Guard, the Liverpool City Police, the East Wavertree Musical Society, Foden's Motor Works Band, the Blackburn Musical Society, the Aviation Works Band and the Birkenhead Male Voice Choir.

Alone among Festival centres of Britain, Liverpool included Music Hall as one of the arts of the theatre. Under the direction of Mr. TD Clarke three all-star bills were presented during the Festival including:- Arthur Askey, Anne Ziegler & Webster Booth, Beryl Orde, Geraldo and his Orchestra, Sonnie Hale, Lucan & McShane and Sid Millward & his Nitwits.

On three evenings there were spectacular displays on the River Mersey. Starting shortly after 8.30 pm a flotilla of ships included ferry boats, tugs, dredgers, salvage vessels, five fast patrol boats of the Royal Navy, which carried out high speed precision manoeuvres.

On 26 July, this was preceded by a display given by two squadrons of the Fleet Air Arm flying from Stretton; a fly-past of Hawker Sea Furies; Blackburn Firebrands and formation aerobatics including a squadron of Seafires.

The final part of the programme each evening commenced at 10.30pm when two trains each of four barges fired the largest display of fireworks in the entire Festival of Britain.

There were three street processions featuring colourful emblems modelled on early Japanese processional features and represented many aspects of the daily life of the region. School children and art students combined in making flowers, animals, fish, railway engines and aeroplanes, all of which were carried high above the heads of the participants.

Each procession had a distinctive theme:- 'Merseyside and Youth', 'Merseyside and the World' and 'Merseyside Resurgent' which was intended to express the faith and determination of the people of a region which suffered greatly in the war.

Sporting events included:- A triangular athletic tournament at the Stanley Stadium, Prescot Road, where world champions from the United States competed against the finest athletes of the AAA and the Northern Counties. Cricket fixtures were arranged by the **Sefton** and Liverpool cricket clubs; a Festival boxing tournament was held at the Liverpool Stadium, Bixteth Street consisting of an inter-city match between Dublin and Liverpool, an inter-divisional match between Manchester and Liverpool, and a number of special challenge bouts; a Championship Swimming Gala was held at the Harold Davies Bath, East Prescot Road, Liverpool, including races between British and Continental champions, also a water ballet display and a water polo match.

Exbibitions included:- 'Daylight on Industry' which was an exhibition designed to show the variety and vigour of Merseyside industry - held in the open air on a blitzed site adjoining Lord Street.

'The Story of Liverpool' in St. George's Hall, was presented jointly by the Corporation and the university. It dealt with the history and development of Merseyside from prehistoric times and concluded with a view of the city in the future. 'Fifty Years of Merseyside Art' was held at Bluecoat Chambers and was divided into two sections - contemporary and retrospective.

'Press Cartoons' an exhibition was held in a gallery at Owen Owen, Clayton Square, of newspaper and magazine cartoons. An exhibition of the work of the 18th century artist, George Stubbs, was held in the newly re-opened Walker Art Gallery - including examples from the Royal collection.

Exhibitions of photography were held at Bluecoat Chambers for professionals and amateurs of the area at Radiant house, Bold Street. An Antique Musical Instruments exhibition was on show at the Rushworth Concert Hall.

Above: **Speke** *New Town was started before the war when 25% of the 5,000 houses were built - they were completed by 1951 with a population of 22,000. Based on this success an even more ambitious project was started at* **Kirkby** *in 1950[LOH]*

Above: *Barker & Dobson was established in Liverpool in 1834 as dealers in high class chocolates and confectionery. By 1860 they had premises in Paradise Street and by 1880 were at 34-36 Duke Street - by 1903 they had moved to Franklin Place off Whitefield Road* **Everton** *and also had four shops in Liverpool*

Feb 2   Liverpool FC record attendance of 61,905 for the FA Cup 4th Round

Feb 7   King George VI died

June 30 Treasures were saved when fire swept through the Queen Anne wing of Croxteth Hall[LDPCE]

Oct 10   Two people were shot dead at Knowsley Hall - Lady Derby and a man servant wounded - a footman was arrested[LDPCE]

Oct 18   The rebuilt St Nicholas' Church consecrated by the Bishop of Liverpool in the presence of the Princess Royal

*Above: Liverpool Corporation Tram No.973 which is seen in St Marys Road, **Garston** in 1952, started service in 1937 and was withdrawn in 1956 - the single-decker bus behind the tram Reg. No.OMX 356 was a Bedford OB/ Duple bought by the Corporation from British Airways*

*Above: Tramcar No.930 is seen at **Aigburgh Vale** on Route No.8 to **Garston** in 1952*

Below: Crowds of people out shopping in Lord Street with Church Street beyond - Bunney's store can be seen in the centre under the two spires on the corner of Whitechapel - there was no trouble parking cars then!

Above: Booth's Wine Stores were founded in Liverpool in 1851 by John Thomas Booth [the great grandfather of the author] with offices in Pownall Square - by 1909 they had seven branches in Liverpool. They were taken over by Bents c.1952 when they had 12 branches throughout Liverpool with cellars in The Albany having just sold off five branches in Wirral

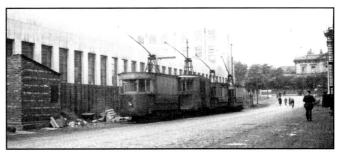

Above: Works and snowplough Tramcars Nos.234, 273,283 & 287 are seen at Edge Lane Works in 1952

1953

Jan 26 The *Empress of Canada* was totally burnt out in Gladstone Dock, Liverpool[LDPCE]

Mar 29 Blackler's new store opened in Elliot Street (*see pg 53*)

May 29 HMS *Sheffield* open to the public in Gladstone Dock

May 30 Coronation Service in all synagogues in Liverpool

May 31 Coronation Service in Liverpool Cathedral and all other churches in Liverpool - Coronation Concert in the Philharmonic Hall - last day for an Exhibition of 'Kings and Queens' at the Walker Art Gallery and also the 'Coronation Exhibition' at the Picton Reference Library

June 1 Planting of Coronation Avenue of Trees in Utting Avenue by the Lord Mayor - March Past by officers and crew of HMS *Sheffield* - official opening of Coronation Gardens in Paradise Street - Schools Festival of Music at Liverpool Stadium with a choir of 1,500 children accompanied by the Merseyside Youth Orchestra - Coronation display by the Liverpool Battalion of the Boy's Brigade in Jericho Lane playing fields

June 2 Queen Elizabeth II Coronation Day
HMS *Sheffield* fired a 21 Gun Salute - concerts throughout the city - Boy Scouts' Coronation Beacons at **Walton** Hall Park; Rice Lane Recreation Ground; Holt's Recreation Ground, **Mossley Hill**; Northumberland Terrace (blitzed site); Otterspool Promenade and **Wavertree** Recreation Ground - Firework Display at Walton Hall Park

June 3 Coronation Swimming Gala at Harold Davies' Baths, **Dovecot** - concerts were held throught the city - basketball demonstration, Lord Street Arena - concert at the Liverpool Stadium by the Philharmonic Orchestra and Choir and the Welsh Choral Union

June 6 Final day of Coronation celebrations with Coronation Procession through the city - fireworks at **Wavertree** Recreation Ground

Above: *The nearest Tramcar No.14 is progressing along Lime Street with St George's Hall in the background - plenty of people, cars, trams and buses can be seen*

Above: *Liverpool Corporation Tram No.762 on the 10B Route is seen in Kensington (Hall Lane) destination Lime Street - built in 1931, re-built in 1938 and withdrawn in 1955*

Above: *Bold Street looking south towards St Luke's Church showing the street decorated for Queen Elizabeth's Coronation on 2 June 1953*

Above: Liverpool Corporation Streamliner Tramcar No.955 is seen under Clubmoor Railway Station bridge - this tram was in service from 1937 to 1955

Above: The open space on the left is where a bombed-out building once stood in Lord Street - the building to the left of the Route No.19 tram is the British Home Stores - the Liver Birds on top of the Liver Building can be seen above the shops

Above: Looking up Parker Street with Clayton Square and Elliot Street beyond

Left: The latest Guinness advert is displayed - attached to the side of the Liverpool Overhead Railway - which was in its last few years - one of the Mersey Tunnel ventilation buildings and the Liver Building is seen above and behind the railway

1954

Mar 6   *Empress of Canada* raised from Gladstone Dock having sunk in January 1953

Mar 13 Official opening of **Litherland** Moss County Primary School by the Earl of Derby

Apr 24 Field-Marshal The Right Honorable The Earl Alexander Of Tunis KG, PC, GCB, GCMG, CSI, DSO, MC was presented with the Freedom of the Borough of **Crosby**

June 27 Holy Cross Church re-opened in Great Crosshall Street (*see photo*) having been damaged by bombing 21 December 1940 it was finally destroyed in the May Blitz of 1941[CofHC]

July 19 Jubilee of Liverpool Cathedral was celebrated[LDPCE]

Oct 22 It was reported that 'Loyal Liverpool salutes the Queen' when she visited Merseyside[LDPCE]

Above: The new Holy Cross Church is pictured in Great Crosshall Street, Liverpool. The first significant date in the history of Holy Cross was 25 March 1849 when a temporary church was opened to accommodate the influx of Catholics following the Irish potato famine. The building housed a cow-house and coal store on the ground floor; on the first floor a rag & bone depot; the second floor was used as a school and the third floor as the temporary church. The new church was opened 14 October 1859 being described as a "Cathedral in Miniature". Adjoining properties were purchased and over the years additions were made. Then on 21 December 1940 the building was severely damaged by enemy action and became a total loss during the May Blitz of 1941. The new church was opened 27 June 1954[CofHC]

Below: Liverpool Corporation Tramcar No.906 - which came into service in 1936, was withdrawn in 1956 - on Route No.10B with Page Moss and London Road on the destination board - seen in Prescot Road, **Old Swan,** where the trams kept to the centre of the road, allowing other vehicles to proceed on the main road without being held up by the trams

Above: Looking down Church Street towards the junction with Whitechapel and Coopers' Building (the tallest building on the left) on the corner of Paradise Street - to the left is a car park on a cleared bomb site - this was the last few years of the Liverpool tram with two seen in the distance compared with four buses

Above: One of the Empress liners berthing at the Liverpool Landing Stage - two trams and four buses can be seen at Pier Head with Wirral in the background

Right: This Experimental Leyland PDRI Bus on hire to Ribble from Leyland (see sign in front window) *was Reg. No.STF 90 - seen at Pier Head - St Nicholas' Church can be viewed beyond the Liverpool Overhead Railway*

Below: This BEA Pionair Class DC3 (Dakota), which had a silver airframe with red trim, can be seen in front of Liverpool's Speke Airport - this type of plane operated on the Isle of Man flight

1955

- Population of Liverpool 786,100[LDPCE]
- Higsons Brewery bottling store opened

Jan 3   The anniversary of Liverpool Diocese[LDPCE]

Jan 22   Ten lives were saved in a Mersey collision in fog in the **Crosby** Channel[LDPCE]

Feb 23   Hundreds of commuters were stranded at Liverpool Exchange Station following a strike of guards at **Southport**[LDPCE]

*Above: Not only the driver and conductor of the last tram on Route 21 to **Aintree** pose for the photographer but four others manage to get in as well in - front or aboard the Liverpool Corporation tram No.167*

Above: *Looking up London Road - the* Odeon *cinema is seen on the right where Gary Cooper was taking the leading role in the film 'Return to Paradise'*

Left: *View of tram No.185 on Route No.14 passing under a train on the Liverpool Overhead Railway- the bus in the background was the mode of transport that would replace both railway and tram within two years as they would both be discontinued with the Overhead Railway being dismantled*

Right: *The Route No.19 Liverpool Corporation Tram is heading along Walton Hall Avenue for Pier Head via Church Street*

SCOTT'S EMPIRE BAKERIES

THE HOME OF GOOD BREAD

Left: *Scott's Empire Bakeries, whose Sunblest Bakery is pictured in Dunnings Bridge Road, Netherton, celebrated their 75th anniversary in 1955. Thomas Scott, flour miller and baker, started the business in 1880 in Great Howard Street, Liverpool. They boasted that their factory in 1955 was one of the most up-to-date and hygienic bakeries in the British Isles and open to visitors - they produced and distributed to their own stores and other outlets throughout Merseyside - the management claimed that they maintained a generous and friendly relationship throughout the area for many years*

Above: *The Booth Line ship* Hubert, *pictured in the River Mersey passing* **Wallasey** *Town Hall, was built in 1955*

1956

May 13   Night bus service started through the Mersey Tunnel - Liverpool and **Birkenhead** buses alternated every three months[LTVol2]

Dec 30   Liverpool Overhead Railway closed[LTVol2]

Above: Pictured in Sefton Park, the octagonal Band Stand, built on an island in 1899, is seen with slender iron columns on a brick base with a pagoda red tiled roof - originally it had a weather vane on top

Left: Pictured in Edge Lane (Rathbone Road), this Liverpool Corporation Tramcar No.SP4 (originally No.646) came into service in 1924 and was withdrawn from normal service in 1952 but was used as a snow plough until 1957

Below: This aerial view of the buildings facing the River Mersey shows the Liverpool Overhead Railway which runs from top left to middle right, before it was demolished in 1957. There are still bomb sites on the right and the Dock Entrance to the Mersey Tunnel is seen to the left of the Liver Building Clock

Left: This postcard of Notre Dame Convent Woolton was posted in 1957

Below: This photograph of the train on the Liverpool Overhead Railway leaving Huskisson Dock, was taken on 2 December 1956 - the line closed later that month on 30 December 1956 and the railway line was dismantled (see also 1957)

Above: Another view taken in the last years of the Liverpool Overhead Railway with Pier Head to the right in front of the Liver building - with over 20 buses in sight

1957

Sept 14 Last Liverpool Corporation tram services withdrawn[RR&FOL]

Sept 23 Work started on removing the Liverpool Overhead Railway structure

JACK SHARP LTD.
SPORTS SPECIALISTS
For all

CYCLE CLOTHING AND
CAMPING EQUIPMENT

36-38 WHITECHAPEL, LIVERPOOL 1.
Telephone: ROYal 4793

Right: The pedestrian is walking next to the stanchions of the Liverpool Overhead Railway which was in the process of being demolished having closed on 30 December 1956

CITY OF LIVERPOOL
C. F. MOTT TRAINING COLLEGE

*Left: This is a multi-view picture postcard of the GF Mott Teacher Training College, Liverpool Road **Huyton**. The centre picture on the top row shows the main building The Hazels which was an impressive red brick building dating back to 1764 and at one time the home of the Pilkington family. The College later became the Liverpool Polytechnic and then part of the John Moores University*

Below: These C & R Garages offered value for money in 1957 - the only drawback, which was not known at the time, was that they were partly made of Asbestos

Below: The new Canadian Pacific liner Empress of England *is pictured in the River Mersey in front of the Liver Building - she was launched in 1957 with accommodation for 160 first class and 898 tourist passengers*

Above: Looking down Church Street towards Lord Street

Above: *Crosville bus on Route No.120 proceeding down Lord street, en route to* **Warrington**

THE STORY OF LIVERPOOL

1207 - 1957

On the occasion of the 750th anniversary of the granting of Liverpool's first charter by King John, this book has been published by the Corporation of Liverpool for presentation to the citizens of all ages in the schools of the City.

Above: *To celebrate Liverpool's 750th Anniversary of the granting of their charter, Liverpool Corporation published the above book,* The Story of Liverpool, *presenting a copy to each school child in Liverpool*

Left: *Last official Liverpool Corporation Tramcar No.293 being escorted along Lime Street by the Police Motor Cyclist - this tram came into service in 1939 and finished on the last day 14 September 1957. Regrettably it is deteriorating in a museum in Maine USA*

ACKNOWLEDGEMENTS

I would like to thank the following people who have either loaned me books or photographs, or given me help and advice in the preparation of this publication:- James Boumphrey, Marilyn Boumphrey, Michael Brocklebank, Joan de Ritter, Anna Graham, Bill Johnstone, Ted Lloyd, Stuart Marsh, TB Maund, John Mills, Mills Media, Albert Nute, David Roberts

By the Same Author:

Yesterday's Wirral No 1 – Neston, Parkgate & Heswall
Yesterday's Wirral No 2 – Birkenhead, Prenton & Oxton
Yesterday's Wirral No 3 – West Kirby & Hoylake
Yesterday's Wirral No 4 – Wallasey & New Brighton
Yesterday's Wirral No 5 – Wallasey, New Brighton & Moreton
Yesterday's Wirral No 6 – Neston, Parkgate & Heswall including Thurstaston & Irby
Yesterday's Wirral No 7 – Birkenhead, Oxton & Prenton including Bidston & Upton
Yesterday's Wirral No 8 – Bebington & Mid Wirral Villages
Yesterday's Wirral No 9 – Ellesmere Port to Bromborough
Yesterday's Wirral Pictorial History 1890 to 1953
Yesterday's Wirral Port Sunlight 1888 to 1953 by Ian Boumphrey and Gavin Hunter
Walking , Cycling & Riding Along the Wirral Way & the Story of the Hooton to West Kirby Railway
Birkenhead at War including Bebington 1939-45 – 84 pages - a War Diary with photographs + list of all those who died
Wirral on the Home Front 1939-45 – This 128 page book covers all of Wirral during WWII adverts & comic postcards in colour

By the Same Publisher:

The Funny Side of Wirral –	Cartoons by Bill Stott
Another Funny Side of Wirral –	Cartoons by Bill Stott
Liverpool –	Cartoons by Bill Stott
Liverpool Home –	Cartoons by Bill Stott
Liverpool 3 –	Cartoons by Bill Stott
The Wirral Country Bus –	TB Maund
The Birkenhead Bus –	TB Maund
The Wallasey Bus –	TB Maund
Shadow to Shadow – History of Bristol Aeroplane Banwell & BAJ –	
Birkenhead Electric Trams –	Charles Rycroft
Railway Stations of Wirral –	Mersey Railway History Group
Murder & Mayhem in Birkenhead –	David Malcolm
More Murder & Mayhem in Birkenhead including Waasey & New Brighton	David Malcolm & Ian Boumphrey
Walking Through the Blitz in the Birkenhead Area –	NHC Tomlinson
The Story of Mariner's Park Wallasey –	Robert Currams & Mike Condon
Birkenhead Park Cricket Club 1846-1996 –	Chris Elston
Medical Matters in Victorian & Edwardian Wallasey –	Dr Richard A Smye
Wallasey at War 1939-45 –	Wallasey Historical Society
Helmets, Handcuffs & Hoses - the Story of the Wallasey Police –	Noel Smith
Helmets, Handcuffs & Hoses - the Story of the Wallasey Fire Brigade –	Noel Smith
Hoylake Racecourse and the beginnings of the Royal Liverpool Golf Club –	John Pinfold
Beachcombers, Buttercreams and Smuggler's Caves - New Brighton & Liverpool in the 1950s – Pepe Ruiz	

I also distribute for several local authors.

For a Free Catalogue of Wirral Publications which includes publications by other local authors (some books are sent Post Free in the UK or post at cost abroad) contact the publisher:
Ian Boumphrey *The Nook* 7 Acrefield Road Prenton Wirral CH42 8LD
or Phone/Fax: 0151 608 7611 or e-mail: ian@yesterdayswirral.co.uk
or visit my Web Site: www.yesterdayswirral.co.uk

WANTED - The author would be interested to view or Buy any old photographs, postcards, ephemera, books, souvenir booklets, guides, old newspapers etc. especially related to Wirral or Liverpool
Also any Gore's, Kelly's or other Directories (including Telephone Directories) pre 1980 especially of Wirral, Liverpool or Cheshire.   Telephone/Fax: 0151 608 7611.
Or e-mail: ian@yesterdayswirral.co.uk